Every Barn Tells A Story

Ann Zemke & Diane Entrikin

ISBN 978-0-9779699-1-3

Graphic Design & Printing by Palmer Printing Company
2902 South 3rd Street, Waite Park, Minnesota 56387

Published by
Crocus Lane Quilts
11060 Amen Circle NE
Blaine, Minnesota 55449

www.crocuslanequilts.com

To our mothers
Gladys Johnson and Betty Hengemuhle

Special thanks
to our husbands John Entrikin and Craig Zemke

A BARN. A QUILT.

Put the two together, and what do you get? It's a "barn quilt," of course! You know, those

colorful quilt blocks you see hanging or painted on barns. Haven't heard of them? Well, it all

started one day when I lightheartedly suggested to my mother that painting a quilt block on our

old tobacco drying barn might improve its drab gray appearance. Fast forward 10 years: barn

quilts, now fashioned into the Quilt Trail, have blossomed in rural America, sprouted in Canada

and grown in numbers beyond my wildest dreams.

I'd like Ann and Diane to tell you the whole story, though, so meander through these pages as

I have done. I hope you'll join the Quilt Trail. Don't have a barn? Consider painting a barn

quilt to hang on a fence at the end of your driveway, as Diane did. Or paint a barn quilt as

a family or community project. Share stories, like the extraordinary ones Ann and Diane have

collected, while you work. You may even be inspired to make one of these beautiful projects they

created with you in mind.

Happy quilting and happy Quilt Trail to you.

Donna Sue Groves

No matter how young or old you are, you have stories to tell. Each of us is a multi-colored and textured patchwork of experiences, momentous occasions and heaps of sentiments. Moreover, we have the power to tap into our ancestors' tales, lessons and ideals.

There are many ways to hand down your stories and family history: through a quilt, a barn, a quilt barn, or even a ball of string. We have collected stories from farm families and shared our own. Some of the stories are about barns, some are about quilts, and some are just for fun. The point is: find a way to tell your story.

We hope you'll find inspiration in the projects we created and the stories we share.

Acknowledgements

This book exists because of the efforts of many accomplished and
kind-hearted people. We extend gratitude to:

Donna Sue Groves, whose Quilt Trail vision has artistically and cleverly redecorated
America's rural landscape. You've warmed us all.

The barn owners, who eagerly shared their extraordinary stories, photos
and historical information. You are the essence of our book.

Kelly Riskedahl, executive director, Grundy County Development Alliance, and Robin Bostrom, executive director,
Fayette County Economic Development. The Grundy County (IA) and Fayette County (IA)
barn quilt projects are remarkable models. Your hospitality is first-class.

Lisa van der Steur, also known as Devil Woman, for her 12-stitches-to-the-inch editorial advice.

Marcy Grant, our cherished friend who prepared tasty meals for us while we sewed,
then tested our patterns and named one of the sampler quilts besides.

Deb Buchholz, who smoothed out our pattern wrinkles with superb technical editing.

Jean Woodson, who offered her perfect piecing skills to test the block pattern with an attitude.

Creative Cut-ups, our beloved quilt group, for supporting us from the beginning to the end.

Bonnie Gibbs, who skillfully quilted Star Promenade and Barn Dance.
Your stunning machine quilting talents are unsurpassed.

Barb Ludvigson, who expertly cross-stitched the Teeple Barn picture.

Sue Rosholt, a special friend and neighbor, who unsuspectingly became our photographer one day.

Mickman Brothers, Inc.
Don and Jamie Kveton
Erin and Dan Holter
Sara Duane

Permissions
• DutchHexSign.com, Corinth, Maine
• Dan Carraco and the Warrick Family Collection
• Julianne Donofrio, Washington, DC
• Janet Doan, Athens Photographic Project
• Donna Sue Groves, Manchester, Ohio
• Shirley Fettkether, Maynard, Iowa
• Patty Schulte, Caledonia, Minnesota
• Jacki Bock, Belmond, Iowa
• Dan and Lisa Sheller, Eldora, Iowa
• Ken and Carol Teeple, Elgin, Illinois
• Debbie Salter Goodwin, author, *Quilted with Love*, Beaverton, Oregon
• The League of Catholic Women, Minneapolis, Minnesota
• Marian Tesdall, Red Wing, Minnesota
• Apron Applause, *The Furrow*, Deere & Company
• Ruth Ratliff, Cedar Falls, Iowa
• St. Peter's Evangelical Lutheran Church Cemetery Association, Union, Minnesota
• Rockford Area Historical Society, Ames-Florida-Stork House, Rockford, Minnesota

Contents

Dedication/Special Thanks 2

Preface 3

Foreword 4

Acknowledgements 5

Barns–Vanishing American Icons 8

History of the Quilt Trail 10

Quilt Barn Stories & Block Patterns

General Directions 13

Contrary Wife 14

Ohio Star 16

Clay's Choice 18

State Fair 20

Bock's Block 22

Gentleman's Fancy 24

Arrowheads 26

Snail's Trail 28

Corn and Beans 30

Card Trick 32

Goose Tracks 34

Variable Star 36

Sister's Choice 38

Log Cabin 40

Bear Paw 41

Crossed Canoes 42

Contrary Husband 43

County Fair 44

Eight Pointed Star 45

Dutchman's Puzzle.................................. 46

Friendship Star...................................... 47

Contrary Wife.. 48

Quilts & Other Projects

Star Promenade.................................... 50

Barn Dance 54

Geese All Around.................................. 58

Broken Stars 60

Twilight.. 62

Roses in the Cabin................................ 64

Paint a Barn Quilt.................................. 69

Apron Applause 71

Smock Apron 72

Embroidered Gingham Apron 76

Teeple Barn Cross Stitch...................... 79

Embroidered Daisy Dishtowel.............. 81

Appliquéd Hand Towel 83

Quilt Label Pocket................................ 85

St. Peter's Evangelical Lutheran Church
and Table Grace.................................... 86

Recipes

Julie's Apple Bread............................... 87

Baked Oatmeal 87

About the Authors

Biographies.. 88

Barns—Vanishing American Icons

No architecture embodies the spirit of American farmers better than their barns. The country's most historic barns are fading from rural landscapes: they are incompatible with contemporary farming, or they are too expensive to maintain or preserve. These grand structures, symbols of the nation's agrarian roots, will soon disappear except in memories and photographs.

The first American barns were sometimes mere mud structures or hillside caverns that early American colonists constructed to provide winter shelter for their animals. As New World pioneers became America's first farmers, they fashioned buildings with distinctive designs and architecture. A barn might reflect Dutch heritage, with a broad gable roof extending low to the ground. Other barns reflected regional attributes, with local materials such as rock used in sturdy stone foundations or timber in solid log structures.

Styles of barns evolved as agricultural colleges began teaching progressive farming methods. The round barn was promoted as costing less and more efficient than traditional rectangular barns: it required fewer building materials and the farmer could work in a continuous circular pattern. Claims of efficiency were exaggerated, however, and this style never became as widespread as promoters had hoped. Another interesting theory, considered folklore at best, is that a round barn was intended to keep the devil from hiding in corners.

The prairie barn, also known as the Western style barn, was built to store enormous amounts of hay and feed for the large cattle herds on Plains state farms. Its characteristic peaked roof above a hayloft eventually gave way to the recognizable gambrel-style roof which expanded storage space even more.

Although barn styles evolved, the color standard of nearly all American barns has remained constant—identifiable barn red. The earliest settlers in the eastern states sealed their barns with an ochre-colored linseed oil derived from the flax crops they grew. Even if barn owners had had access to colored paint then, it would have been considered lavish and sensational to paint anything so utilitarian as a barn.

Farmers in the north didn't have access to the same oils as their eastern counterparts; if they wanted to preserve their barn's wood, then they needed to formulate a product from the resources available. Practical farmers found that when they combined ferrous oxide, otherwise known as rust, with skim milk and lime, it made a product that hardened quickly and lasted for years. Rust, in addition to being abundant on farms, is poisonous to fungi, including moss and mold, which trap moisture in wood and speed decay. Although the homemade paint formula produced more of a burnt-orange color than the bright fire-engine red we often see today, early American farmers created the recognizable color named "barn red."

In the mid-19th century, as commercial paint became more readily available and affordable, farmers began to decorate their barns and stables much as they decorated their houses. The Pennsylvania Dutch, a settlement of German immigrants in southeastern Pennsylvania, started painting bright circular signage to adorn their barns. The word "Dutch" in "Pennsylvania Dutch," came from "Deutschland," the German word for Germany.

Like many New World settlers, these German immigrants brought their traditions with them to their new homes. Floral designs and geometric patterns—which decorated birth certificates, family Bibles, marriage certificates and quilts—found a place in colorful folkart signage as well. The six-pointed star design, painted within a circle, was considered a form of hex sign by superstitious types.

The word "hex" has two possible meanings: The German word for six is *sechs*, which sounded like *hex* to English speaking neighbors. The German word *hexe* means "witch." Some people believed so-called hex signs warded off evil influences and brought fertility to farms, while others viewed them only as colorful decorations. The latter interpretation is more likely; the same "hex" motifs frequently appeared in period quilts.

The first American signage of this type was rather simplistic in its design. It wasn't until the commercial hex sign business developed around 1940 that these emblems were purposefully and intricately painted with connotations such as luck and hospitality, as identified by the shamrock and the pineapple.

For decades, hex signs have drawn masses of curious tourists to Lancaster County, Pennsylvania. They purchase these colorful decorations on a wide array of goods produced by hundreds of local craftsmen. As a result, economic development and tourism have flourished in the region, even as this interesting aspect of American design has been preserved.

At the turn of the 20th century, barns took on a new colorful appearance when Bloch Brothers Tobacco Company realized that rather than constructing new billboards, they could use existing structures to advertise their new product—Mail Pouch Tobacco. The Bloch brothers, who began manufacturing cigars in 1879 as a sideline to Samuel Bloch's wholesale grocery business, discovered that leftover stogie clippings could be flavored, packaged and sold. The product's paper packaging resembled a mail pouch, hence the name Mail Pouch Tobacco.

 The Bloch Brothers' sales force began their outdoor advertising campaign by approaching farmers for advertising space on—what else—their barns. Farmers got their barns painted for free and received additional compensation: free tobacco, magazine subscriptions and small cash payments. Farmers eagerly signed up, and the Bloch Brothers' advertising campaign flourished. The greatest concentration of these barns-cum-billboards was near the company's home in West Virginia, Ohio, Pennsylvania, southern New York and western Maryland.

A private contractor engaged by Bloch Brothers in 1925 hired six "barnstorm painters" to paint Mail Pouch signs on barns: two men per Ford Model T truck, accessorized with side curtains. The typical Mail Pouch barn was painted black with yellow and white lettering, which encouraged passersby to "Chew Mail Pouch Tobacco—Treat Yourself to the Best." Red barns were rarely chosen for painted advertisements because they faded more rapidly than black barns and required more maintenance.

Mail Pouch sign painters came and went over the years until Harley Warrick, the last and most prolific Mail Pouch sign painter, came along. Warrick's sign painting interest had been piqued in the 1940s when he watched a Mail Pouch crew paint an advertisement on  his family's Londonderry, Ohio, barn. Little did he imagine then. that during a 45-year career he would paint over 20,000 "Chew Mail Pouch Tobacco" barn signs. Within a few days of returning home from the service in World War II, Warrick greeted the Mail Pouch painters, who had returned to repaint the familiar slogan on his family's barn. Warrick expressed an interest in learning the trade—and left later that day as part of the team.

Warrick painted Mail Pouch signs free-hand. With experience he could complete a barn in about four hours. He always began each barn sign by painting the 'E' in the word "CHEW." Then he painted the 'H' and the 'W', which spelled out his initials "H.E.W." Warrick said he liked to "sign" his work before he began, although he did write his signature at the bottom corner of each barn he painted.

Looking to the future, in 1990 Warrick tried to train his replacement. The new sign painter stayed on the job little more than a year.

The number of Mail Pouch barns plunged dramatically beginning in 1965 when Congress passed the Highway Beautification Act. This law called for controls on outdoor advertising, including removal of certain types of signage along interstate or primary highways and elimination or screening of junkyards. Condemned as eyesores, Mail Pouch Tobacco barns along America's interstate highway system met this definition and were painted over or demolished. Now recognized as icons of a time gone by, fewer than 2,000 Mail Pouch barns remain today.

References:
• Sloane, Eric, American Barns and Covered Bridges, New York, NY: Wilfred Funk, Inc., 2003, 65-69.
• Butterbaugh, Kelly Ann, "America's Unicorns: Mail Pouch Barns." Iowa Barn Journal, 2006, 11.2.
• Stambaugh, Perry, "A Vanishing Rural Icon." Penn Lines, 1999, Vol. 34 No. 3, 18, 20.
• Beck Paprock, Sherry, "Out Standing in the Fields." Country Magazine, 1994, 18.

History of the Quilt Trail

Growing up in West Virginia, Donna Sue Groves played a car game that her mother Maxine Groves created to pass the time on family road trips. The first person in the car to see a certain kind of barn received points based on the barn's architecture, style or color. Barns that displayed painted commands such as **Chew Mail Pouch Tobacco** *and* **Drink Royal Crown Cola** *drew a 10 point bonus—but only if the sign was readable. A barn adorned with a rare and coveted Pennsylvania Dutch hex sign returned an enormous 50 point premium.*

Gazing at the drab barn with her mother one day, Donna Sue decided that maybe the unappealing structure just needed to be jazzed up a bit, perhaps brightened with a splash of color. Then and there, Donna Sue promised her mother—a fifth generation quilter and a master quilter—that she would paint a single quilt block on the side of the barn. That would perk it up nicely.

Time slipped away and the tired barn got grayer, silently reproaching Donna Sue for the promise she had made to her mother in 1989 but had not yet kept. Almost a dozen years later, when some friends offered to help Donna Sue at last paint the quilt block on the barn, she said, "If we're going to paint one quilt block, then we should paint several of them."

Donna Sue, who had made a 20-year career working with non-profit organizations and artists to promote community development, imagined the tremendous possibilities of a "quilt trail"—a driving route that would attract visitors to Adams County, stimulate the local economy and pull the community and its artisans together. "I never saw the project as an end-all be-all. I envisioned it as an addition to assets the community already had, such as its beautiful landscapes and talented artists."

Donna Sue, the quilt barn concept visionary, pulled together community volunteers—grassroots people—to form the Adams County Ohio Quilt Barn Committee. This group designed and created the quilt barn project model now used almost everywhere quilt trails exist. As committee chair, she gave encouragement from the sidelines and quietly made suggestions to the group as she walked around the edges of the meeting room. "I didn't create the model," Donna Sue affirms. "I was just the glue."

The car game, which seemed to be only about keeping the kids occupied, was really much more. The Groves family car became a classroom on wheels as the conversation covered topics from history and geography to anthropology and architecture. Without realizing it, Donna Sue was learning about barn structure, settlement patterns, who the Pennsylvania Dutch were, why barns are painted red, and so much more.

In 1989, Donna Sue and her mother moved from West Virginia to an Adams County, Ohio, farm with an uninteresting tobacco barn on the property. The dark gray color of the barn absorbed the sun's rays, raising the barn's internal temperature and drying the tobacco leaves inside more quickly.

The first painted quilt square, appropriately an Ohio Star, was not painted on Donna Sue's gray barn, which became grayer still.

Instead, it was revealed at the 2001 Lewis Mountain Olde Thyme Herb Fair in Winchester, Ohio. The overwhelmingly positive reaction from the press and the thousands in attendance at the fair made Donna Sue realize "we were on to something big." She never dreamed the concept would spread like wildfire across the United States. Rather, she was thinking about other communities: how to provide them with the information they needed to implement their own quilt trail projects and tweak the concept based on their local assets.

It is estimated that more than 3,200 painted quilt blocks decorate barns in 30 states. The numbers continue to grow. The phenomenon has even gone international: Canadians are displaying painted quilt blocks too.

There is a joyful simplicity in displaying a single painted quilt block on a barn or a wall, but the quilt barn project is about so much more than that. It's about giving people the opportunity to do simple things that can have an astonishing impact. Whole communities are gathering to paint blocks, recalling old-fashioned quilting bees (which still take place today, although far less often than they used to). Block by block, these individuals, families and towns are weaving a fabric with the potential to warm us all.

Donna Sue said that the Quilt Trail is something solid she will have accomplished in her lifetime, one that will live on past her.

"I hope that someday there's a little girl and a little boy in the back seat of a car, and they aren't connected to anything electronic, and as they look out the window they say, 'Mom, what was that?' And their mom will reply, 'Maybe we'll see another one.'" Or perhaps a painted quilt block on a barn will spark a conversation or encourage them to think of design and color, or they may even be inspired to explore the arts.

So what is the correct terminology for this endeavor anyway? Some people call them *quilt barns* while others may describe them as *barn quilts*. Donna Sue says that she always used quilt barns because her focus was on quilting, and the barn was the palette. But it's a moot point, because it's called the Quilt Trail now. And if you look carefully, you will find painted quilt blocks not only on barns but on fences, in trailer parks, and even in a few campgrounds. Like seeds growing in farm fields, they're popping up all over.

In 2003, Donna Sue at last fulfilled her promise to her mother, when she commissioned a Snail's Trail block to be painted on their old tobacco drying barn.

A Special Story from Donna Sue

Donna Sue Groves never gave much thought to quilts when she was growing up, although they were an everyday part of her life. For instance, there was likely to be a quilt on the quilting frame, or a group of women gathered to piece a quilt, when she visited her grandmas' houses as a child. Quilts were practical items which were made to be used—just another part of the bed.

Then one day on a visit to Grandma Groves's house, Donna Sue had an awakening. That day Grandma Groves instructed Donna Sue to pick three pretty maple leaves from the yard. Although Donna Sue initially questioned her grandma's instructions, she went out to the yard, selected three colorful leaves, and brought them back to her grandma. Again and again, Donna Sue asked her grandma what she intended to do with the leaves, but the elderly lady would only reply, "You'll see."

Donna Sue's grandma made templates from the carefully selected leaves, cut the designs from fabric, and then appliquéd them onto a quilt top. Cleverly and skillfully, Grandma Groves captured the unique design of an ordinary but beautiful piece of nature to craft a quilt. Donna Sue says it was on that day, when her grandma asked her to pick maple leaves, that she first realized quilt making is truly an art form. Donna Sue says, "I experience something very powerful when I look at or hold my special quilt."

Stories &
Quilt Blocks

Half Square Triangles

1. Cut 1 square of each color; layer RST *(right sides together)*.

2. Mark diagonal line, as shown.

3. Stitch ¼" from the marked line. Repeat on other side of marked line.

4. Cut on marked line, resulting in two half square triangle units.

5. Press seams toward dark fabric.

Flying Geese

1. Layer 1 gold square on red rectangle RST.

2. Mark a diagonal line, as shown.

3. Stitch on line.

4. Fold and press square toward corner; trim away middle layer of fabric.

5. Layer another gold square on other end of rectangle.

6. Mark a diagonal line, as shown.

7. Stitch on line.

8. Fold and press square toward corner; trim away middle layer of fabric.

Square in a Square

1. Sew long edge of triangle to top and bottom of square centering on square.

2. Press both triangles away from center square.

3. Sew triangles to both sides, centering as before and press away from center square.

Y-Seam

1. Mark a dot in the corner ¼" from sides of triangle.

2. Start at outer (bottom) edge, stitch diamond pieces together, using a ¼" seam. End seam at dot and backstitch. **Do not stitch beyond dot.**

3. Sew seam #2 in direction of arrow. Stop and backstitch at dot.

4. Stitch seam #3 in direction of arrow, backstitching at dot, then proceed stitching to outer edge.

5. Press seam #1 open. Press seams #2 & #3 toward diamonds.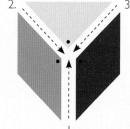

Bits and Pieces

Read all directions first.

Helpful Hint
When preparing to sew blocks with many bias edges, such as Corn and Beans and County Fair, spray fabric with (a good coat of) spray starch before cutting and press. This will aid in preventing stretching of the bias edges.

Seam Allowance
Seam allowance is ¼" unless stated otherwise.

Pressing
Press seam allowances to one side, in direction of arrows.

RST – right sides together

WOF – width of fabric

RSO – right side out

Finished Measurements
All blocks in Barn Dance and Star Promenade are 12" x 12" finished. Unfinished block size is 12½" x 12½". (Exception: the center block in Barn Dance is 18" x 18" finished.)

Marking and Cutting
– – – – – – Indicates stitching line

————— Indicates cutting line

Borders
Although the amounts given for borders are mathematically correct, you may have to adjust the length of your borders to fit your pieced center, due to variances in the ¼" seam allowance.

All knowledgeable basketball fans worth their salt know that "Vets" Auditorium is in Des Moines, Iowa, and "Fetts" Auditorium is in Maynard, Iowa. While the auditoriums may have similar sounding names, they are very dissimilar places.

Veterans Memorial Auditorium (aka Vets Auditorium)—home to Iowa boys and girls state high school basketball and wrestling tournaments from 1995 until 2005—is a 14,700 seat arena built to honor Polk County's World War II veterans. Fett's Auditorium, which has no seating, is a barn on Shirley and Clete Fettkether's farm built in 1958 to house and milk cows. Several decades later, when the Fettkethers stopped milking, the cows were moved out, the floor was swept clean for the first time ever, and a basketball hoop was installed inside the barn. Then, a second hoop was installed, and the vintage barn became a makeshift basketball arena where Clete Fettkether enjoyed playing hoops with his children Matt, Jamie and Kristi ... but only after chores were done.

While basketball is *supposed* to be played on carefully marked and maintained hardwood courts, it didn't matter much to Matt Fettkether and his basketball buddies who took pure pleasure in playing the sport. Matt's mom Shirley took pleasure in the sport too, but rather from the reassuring sound of the bouncing basketball, which she could hear from inside her nearby farm house.

Matt and his friends went on to play for the Blue Devils basketball team at West Central High School in Maynard. Matt's class of slightly more than 40 students proudly represented their school in the 1995 and 1996 Class 1A Iowa boys state basketball tournaments.

And it all began in a barn.

Shirley learned about Fayette County's Quilt Barn project from her sister, Rose Kalb, who works at the Oelwein Chamber of Commerce. Shirley and Rose worked hard to paint the block perfectly. As Shirley said teasingly, "After all, cars are moving at only 60 miles an hour past our place," which is located directly across from Highway C33.

Matt Fettkether, Kristi (Fettkether) Purdy and Jamie Fettkether presented with their father's restored Farmall Tractor. Restoration completed by Ron Kalb, brother-in-law and best friend of Clete Fettkether who died in 1989.

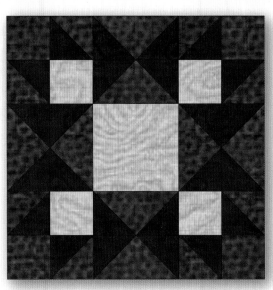

12" x 12" finished

Materials:

- **Gold** (¼ yard)
- **Red** (¼ yard)
- **Blue** (¼ yard)

Cutting Instructions:

Cut 4 – 2½" x 2½"
Cut 1 – 4½" x 4½"

Cut 16 – 2½" x 2½"
Use for Flying Geese.
Cut 4 – 2⅞" x 2⅞"
Use for half square triangles.

Cut 4 – 2½" x 2½"
Cut 8 – 2½" x 4½"
Cut 4 – 2⅞" x 2⅞"
Use for half square triangles.

Please refer to General Directions, page 13, for half square triangle units and Flying Geese used in this block.

 Make 8   Make 8

Block Construction:

1. Row 1 – Sew together, as shown.
2. Row 2 – Sew together, as shown.
3. Row 3 – Sew together, as shown.
4. Row 4 – Sew together, as shown.
5. Row 5 – Sew together, as shown.
6. Press seams in direction of ⇄.
7. Sew Rows 1, 2, 3, 4 & 5 together.
8. Press finished block.

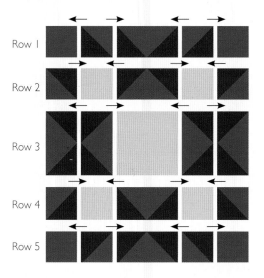

Individuals share their life stories and family history in journals, photographs, tape recordings, videos, or even through the blocks of a quilt. But inside a gigantic ball of string? Clair Campbell, a crop farmer from Hawkeye, Iowa, came up with a novel way to record his life and times.

It seems every time Clair opened a feedsack, he saved the bag's string by wrapping it around the matchbox he always carried in his pocket. Clair's son Bob recalls evenings watching his father unwind the string from the matchbox and carefully *rewind* it into a ball. But the rewinding took place only after Clair had added handwritten notes or a family photograph to the construction—which eventually grew to the size of a basketball.

In 2005, Bob and Trudy Campbell were planning a fishing vacation with their three grown children. Forward-thinking Trudy thought the family might need a rainy day activity, so she packed Clair's huge ball of string along with the fishing gear and provisions. Trudy wanted to unwind the ball.

She didn't realize that, as family members carefully unwound string from the very old ball, they would also be unwinding their family history, piece by piece. Clair had kept the ball of string *as his journal* through the years. He wrote tidbits about the day, recorded significant family happenings or weather events or crop reports, and secreted his entries inside a giant ball of string.

Five years have passed. The Campbells continue to unwind the ball, but only at gatherings when the entire family is present. They're recording their own family history as they proceed, and then are rewinding the string and the pieces of history back into another ball. Now at the halfway point, they can't imagine what Clair's first entry in the string journal will be.

The Ohio Star quilt block is painted red, blue and gold, the North Fayette Community District school colors.

Like three generations before him, Bob Campbell has raised livestock and grown mostly crops of corn and beans for 41 years on the Fayette County land that his great-grandfather Robert purchased from a Civil War widow in 1880. Soon, Bob and his wife Trudy plan to transfer the land to their son Kevin, a fifth generation Campbell farmer. As Bob says, "farming has started to interfere with fishing," his first love—next to Trudy, of course.

12" × 12" finished

Materials:

- **Floral** (5" scrap)
- **Gold** (6" scrap)
- **Red** (¼ yard)
- **Green** (¼ yard)

Cutting Instructions:

 Cut 1 – 4½" × 4½"

 Cut 1 – 5¼" × 5¼"

 Cut 2 – 5¼" × 5¼"

 Cut 1 – 5¼" × 5¼"
Cut 4 – 4½" × 4½"

Quarter Square Triangle

1. Layer one red and one green square RST. Referring to General Directions, make HST. Press toward red.

2. Layer one red and one gold square RST. Referring to General Directions, make HST. Press toward red.

3. Layer one red and green HST and one red and gold HST, RST. Seams will be parallel and red triangles opposite.

4. Mark diagonal line perpendicular to seam. Stitch and cut as for HST, resulting in two QST.

5. Repeat Step 4 for a total of four QST.

Block Construction:

1. Row 1 – Sew together, as shown.
2. Row 2 – Sew together, as shown.
3. Row 3 – Sew together, as shown.
4. Press seams in direction of ⇄ .
5. Sew Rows 1, 2 & 3 together.
6. Press finished block.

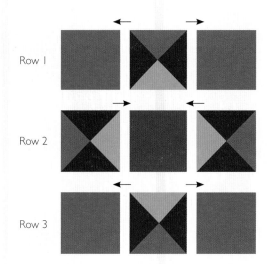

John and Patty Schulte
Caledonia, Minnesota

Patty Schulte doesn't claim sewing quilts as one of her many talents. But her mother and sisters are both quilters, so Patty says quilt making must be in her genes.

One day Patty wondered: "What would my mom and sisters think if I surprised them by making a quilt?" Not a traditional cloth quilt, but a single brightly colored quilt block painted on wood and hung on the 100 year-old Schulte barn. Patty and her family live in Caledonia, Minnesota, where residents have access to a community "paint pool" they can use to create colorful quilt blocks. Patty chose the Clay's Choice pattern to recreate in wood, because it reminded her of the windmill that stands near the family barn. "The painted quilt block," says Patty, "is a neat decoration that I can enjoy every day. Passersby like it too."

On a typical day, the alarm wakes Patty and John Schulte at 3:40 am. Milking their 250 dairy cows commences by 4:00 am. Patty, who every so often works as a milker, also serves as a tractor driver in the fall and all-round helping hand when needed. Early on someone cautioned Patty, "Don't ever learn how to milk!" She heeded the advice for awhile but sympathetically gave in when more help was needed. "I don't really mind the work," she says kindly. The Schultes grow corn, soybeans and hay on the more than 1,000 acres John owns with his brother and another 340 acres that they rent.

The Schulte family farm, homesteaded by John's great-grandfather in the late 1800s, is strategically nestled between the rolling hills that are typical of the topography in the southeastern corner of Minnesota. Patty says the original farm buildings were probably situated that way to shelter them from the bitter winter winds and driving snow. The much newer milking parlor the Schultes built in 2007 is located just beyond the original buildings.

Patty knows firsthand that it can be a long, cold, dark and uphill hike to milk the cows. She allows that she occasionally drives the car from the house to the milking parlor. But who can blame her? The outside temperature may drop to 30 degrees below zero (or colder) in the winter months when the wind is howling.

Patty and John Schulte are the parents of three teenagers. Taylor, Samuel and Brennan all help with farm chores when they're not in school or playing sports. They also helped paint portions of the quilt block.

Patty, who thoroughly enjoyed painting—not sewing—her first quilt block, is considering painting another. Watch for a colorful gallery of quilts hanging at the Schulte farm in Caledonia.

12" × 12" finished

Materials:

- **Brown** (¹/₈ yard)
- **Gold** (¹/₈ yard)
- **Tan** (¹/₈ yard)

Cutting Instructions:

Cut 4 – 3½" × 3½"
Cut 2 – 3⁷/₈" × 3⁷/₈"
Use for half square triangles.

Cut 4 – 3⁷/₈" × 3⁷/₈"
Use for half square triangles.

Cut 4 – 3 ½" × 3 ½"
Cut 2 – 3⁷/₈" × 3⁷/₈"
Use for half square triangles.

Please refer to General Directions, page 13, for half square triangles, used in this block.

 Make 4   Make 4

Block Construction:

1. Row 1 – Sew together, as shown.
2. Row 2 – Sew together, as shown.
3. Row 3 – Sew together, as shown.
4. Row 4 – Sew together, as shown.
5. Press seams in direction of ⇄.
6. Sew Rows 1, 2, 3 & 4 together.
7. Press finished block.

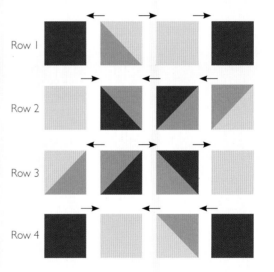

Bud and Belva Gallagher
Caledonia, Minnesota

Francis "Bud" and Belva Gallagher live in a house on the farm that his great–grandfather homesteaded.
The house was built in 1877, and its "new" addition was built in 1929.

Bud's great-grandfather William Gallagher and his brother were among the throngs who left Ireland in the mid-1800s for opportunity in the United States. While in New York, the young brothers were accidentally separated, never to find one another again. From New York, William traveled to Ohio and eventually to Galena, Illinois. Every spring for several years, he left his young family in Galena and ventured alone to Lansing, Iowa, on a Mississippi riverboat. From there he rode horseback about 40 miles to Caledonia, Minnesota, where he spent the warm months building a log cabin, returning in the fall to his family in Galena. The cabin was finally complete in 1860, and William moved his family to Minnesota. Other settlers had built cabins close by, which offered a feeling of community and safety from Indians who lived in the nearby Winnebago Valley.

Bud's grandfather remained on the land that his great-grandfather homesteaded. He grew wheat, which he harvested and then hauled 25 miles east to LaCrosse, Wisconsin—across the Mississippi River. Farmers had to wait patiently until winter to sell their grain so they could cross the river when it was frozen solid enough to withstand the weight of the horse-drawn, grain-filled wagons.

Dianne Welscher, the Gallaghers' daughter, with the help of a friend, painted the bright quilt block which is displayed on the farm's corn crib, built in 1949. Their objective in displaying the quilt block was to contribute to the county barn quilt project and make barn quilt tours more interesting.

Bud and Belva Gallagher, along with their sons, milk 125 dairy cows on their 950 acre farm, where they also grow crops for feed. Bud says that nowadays many dairy farmers hire a dairy nutritionist to help them ascertain the best combination of feed in order to achieve optimum milk production. Bud, however, prefers his own feed theory: he calls it "by guess and by gosh," and it has worked satisfactorily for him over several decades.

Bud is the proud owner of an eye-catching cruet collection, now numbering over 60 unique pieces beautifully displayed in a glass-doored hutch. He started collecting cruets because they reminded him of his mother, who always set one (probably filled with vinegar at his Irish father's request) on the dining table.

Bud's grandfather donated this stained glass window to the Catholic church in Freeburg, Minnesota, to honor his parents. When the deteriorating church was torn down, Bud and Belva purchased the window. The remainder of the window was crafted into keepsakes for their seven children.

It's doubtful that the Gallaghers will ever move off the farm. After all, if they moved to town, where would Belva drive her four-wheeler?

12" × 12" finished

Materials:

✤ **Red** (⅛ yard)
✤ **Green** (⅛ yard)
✤ **Medium Green** (¼ yard)

Cutting Instructions:

Cut 1 – 3⅜" × 3⅜"
Cut 6 – 2⅞" × 2⅞"
Use for half square triangles.

Cut 6 – 2⅞" × 2⅞"
Use for half square triangles.

Cut 2 – 2⅞" × 2⅞"
Cut both once diagonally.
Use for Square in a Square.

Cut 4 – 2½" × 4½"
Cut 4 – 2½" × 2½"
Cut 8 – 2⅞" × 2⅞"
Use for half square triangles.

Please refer to General Directions, page 13, for half square triangles and Square in a Square, used in this block.

  Make 1

• Layer four 2⅞" × 2⅞" red squares with four 2⅞" × 2⅞" medium green squares, RST. Make 8

• Layer four 2⅞" × 2⅞" green squares with four 2⅞" × 2⅞" medium green squares, RST.   Make 8

• Layer two 2⅞" × 2⅞" red squares with two 2⅞" × 2⅞" green squares, RST. Make 4

Block Construction:

1. Row 1 – Sew together, as shown.
2. Row 2 – Sew together, as shown.
3. Row 3:
   • Sew center block (Square in a Square).
   • Sew two half square triangles together then add them to each side of center square.
   • Add rectangles to each end, as shown.
4. Row 4 – Sew together, as shown.
5. Row 5 – Sew together, as shown.
6. Press seams in direction of ⇄ .
7. Sew Rows 1, 2, 3, 4 & 5 together.
8. Press finished block.

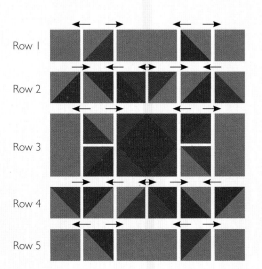

Row 1

Row 2

Row 3

Row 4

Row 5

Harold and Mary Bock raised 10 children on their 360 acre farm in Belmond, Iowa. According to Jacki Bock, her in-laws had a farm that was a home—not only to grow up in, but to return to.

The haymow was a special place to build forts, play hide and seek with visiting cousins, enjoy the kittens or just spend some quiet time. One day, one of the Bock children did the unthinkable: he lit a match in the haymow. Even though no damage was done, the incident served as an important learning opportunity for all of the Bock children—most especially the culprit who had to sit on the front steps of the house, lighting match after match and blowing them out one by one.

On a stormy night in 1998, the Bock family barn was destroyed by strong straight line winds, possibly even a tornado. While the much loved barn may be gone, the fond memories live on.

Jacki Bock created the custom Bock block as a Christmas gift to Mary, who never got to see it. She died the week before Christmas in 2007. The barn quilt was installed on a metal farm building at the family farm where Denise and Mark Bock now live, and where Ken Bock works with his brother.

Each color of Jacki's custom block represents a part of Harold and Mary's lives. White in the block's center represents Harold and Mary, the solid foundation of the family. They taught their children how to work hard, be honest and honor family.

Six pink rectangles surrounding the white center represent the Bock daughters. Four blue star points represent the four Bock sons. Green squares in the corners stand for their livelihood: hogs and cattle, corn and beans.

The four large yellow triangles stand for the more than four decades Harold and Mary lived on the farm, and the four years Mary remained on the farm alone after Harold's sudden death in 2003.

Harold and Mary Bock were proud of their daughter-in-law Jacki, a registered nurse and avid quilter who is always ready to help someone who needs it. Jacki has reconsidered requests for help from her husband Ken, however. Once when Jacki was helping him with some heavy lifting, Ken commented, "Sure could use one more of me and one less of you."

Original Bock barn before and after the 1998 storm.

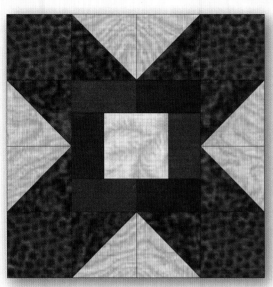

12" × 12" finished

Materials:

White (4" × 4")
❖ **Light pink** (4" × 6")
❖ **Dark pink** (4" × 6")
❖ **Blue** (1/8 yard)
❖ **Green** (1/8 yard)
❖ **Yellow** (1/8 yard)

Cutting Instructions:

Cut 1 – 3 ½" × 3 ½"

Cut 3 – 2" × 3 ½"

Cut 3 – 2" × 3 ½"

Cut 8 – 3 ½" × 3 ½"
Use for Flying Geese.

Cut 4 – 3 ½" × 3 ½"

Cut 4 – 3 ½" × 6 ½"

Please refer to General Directions, page 13, for Flying Geese used in this block.

Make 4

Block Construction:

1. Sew Row 1, as shown.
2. Sew Row 2:
   - Sew one light pink and one dark pink rectangle together, as shown.
   - Sew one light pink and one dark pink rectangle on each side of center square.
   - Sew one light pink and one dark pink rectangle together, as shown.
   - Join above units to form center square.
   - Add a yellow/blue Flying Geese unit to each side of center square.
3. Sew Row 3, as shown.
4. Press seams in direction of ⇄ .
5. Sew Rows 1, 2 & 3 together.
6. Press finished block.

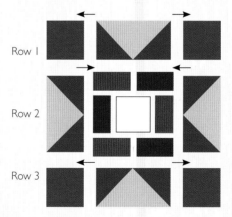

Row 1

Row 2

Row 3

John and Elaine Burg
Caledonia, Minnesota

John Burg and his 11 siblings grew up on the farm that his great-great-grandfather, originally from Luxembourg, homesteaded in 1864. Back then the family raised beef cattle and crops on their farm— a good thing, too, because they usually needed to slaughter at least five large steers every year to keep the growing family fed. Although retired from farming, John and his wife Elaine still live on a farm they purchased in the 1970s, next to the farm where John was raised.

Strip farming

Farmers in the hilly farmland surrounding Caledonia practice strip farming, a method of closely alternating crops such as beans and alfalfa with corn. This planting technique is typically used when the grade of the land is too steep or too long, or when other types of farming may not adequately prevent soil erosion, especially during periods of heavy rain. Farmers plant their crops following the contour of the land, so they can always drive their tractors on level ground. A visiting minister who observed the curvy rows of crops asked, "How do you ever find your way home?"

Elaine and John met on the first Monday of their senior year of high school. They started dating on Friday and have been together ever since: 47 years. In the winter months they escape to sunny Arizona, where John says his John Deere cap is "like fly paper." Farmers run to greet him when they see the traditional green and gold John Deere colors that John wears proudly.

When they're in Caledonia, the Burgs take pleasure in visiting with the onlookers who stop to gaze at the multi-colored quilt block on their white barn. When asked why the barn is painted white, John answers with no hesitation: "Because it was always painted white."

Bright colors and barn quilt block designs had captured Elaine's attention while she was surfing on the Internet one day. She thought, "Now that's something I can do." Constructing and painting the quilt block on two 4' X 8' sheets of plywood was considerably easier than hanging the heavy wooden pieces in place, which Elaine left to John while she gave explicit directions from her comfortable lawn chair nearby. Although not a fabric quilter, she did know how important it is to make sure all the corners and points in the block match…exactly!

Records show that in 1898 Frank Burg, John's grandfather, paid $6.71 property tax on the 200 acres he owned.

24

12" x 12" finished

Materials:

- ❖ **Medium Red** (5" × 5" scrap)
- ❖ **Gold** (¼ yard)
- ❖ **Red** (⅛ yard)
- ❖ **Blue** (¼ yard)

Cutting Instructions:

 Cut 1 – 4½" × 4½"

 Cut 1 – 5¼" × 5¼"
Cut twice diagonally.
Use for Square in a Square.

 Cut 8 – 3⅜" × 3⅜"
Use for Flying Geese.

 Cut 4 – 3⅜" × 6⅛"

 Cut 2 – 4⅞" × 4⅞"
Cut once diagonally.

 Cut 1 – 5¼" × 5¼"
Cut twice diagonally.

Please refer to General Directions, page 13, for Flying Geese and Square in a Square, used in this block.

Make 4   Make 1

Block Construction:

1. Unit 1
   - Sew center block (Square in a Square).
   - Add a Flying Geese unit to each end of center. Press seams outward.
   - Add a large triangle to each Flying Geese unit, centering the long edge of triangle on Flying Geese unit. Press seams outward.
2. Unit 2
   - Sew a small triangle on each end of two remaining Flying Geese units. Press seam toward triangle. Then add large triangle, as shown. Press seam outward.
3. Unit 3
   - Repeat directions as in Unit 2.
4. Press finished block.

Unit 1   Unit 2

Unit 3

Speck Untiedt called his unsuspecting girlfriend Charlotte Barfels from Navy boot camp and said, "Get your blood test—we're gonna get married." With that the young sailor returned to Beaman, Iowa, where his parents Happy and Alice Untiedt owned Untiedt Dairy Farm. The couple married at the church parsonage in 1943.

Word of the marriage traveled quickly through the small town of Beaman, a pleasant rural community situated in the heart of Iowa's richest farming country. Young people in town shivareed the newlyweds by making lots of commotion and knocking on the house door where close family members were enjoying a wedding dinner served by Speck's mother. As tradition goes, revelers expect a treat to cease their commotion, so Speck's father Happy asked the local grocer to open his shop so he could purchase candy bars.

Speck returned to camp for Navy mechanic training before shipping out to the South Pacific. Charlotte, a self-admitted "greenhorn" who had never even been on a train, traveled to Champaign, Illinois, to be with her new husband for six short weeks.

When the young sailor was overseas, Charlotte's only communication with him was V-mail, short letters which were censored with a line or two cut out; it was information that the Navy thought shouldn't be shared. Charlotte wanted to know where Speck was, and she was confident that he wanted her to know, so she read his censored letters carefully watching for code. Finally Speck wrote, "How is Tom Sims' son?" Charlotte was quick to figure out that the man Speck was referring to was named Russell Sims. With that, she concluded that Speck was stationed in the Russell Islands, South Pacific.

Speck and Charlotte's daughter Judy Untiedt was 14 months old before she met her father. While Speck was away, Charlotte would ask their little girl "Where's Daddy?" At that, Judy would point to her daddy's picture.

Upon his return, Speck took over the family's dairy farm, which sold Grade A milk for 50 years. Speck's father hand milked the cows daily, and then delivered bottled milk in a wagon pulled by Blossom the horse, who kept milk delivery on a tight schedule. If Happy visited too long with a customer on his route, Blossom moved on without him.

Speck bought one milking machine when he returned home and many years later built a milking parlor for 60 cows. The dairy he and Charlotte ran was demanding. Milking the cows had to be done, no matter what, so their lives revolved around the dairy. In the evening while their parents milked, Susan, the second of three daughters, prepared supper as Judy and Ann tended to the calves and chickens. Charlotte and Speck loved to go to dances with their friends. But no matter how late they went to bed on Saturday night, they still awoke at 5:00 am to milk the cows.

"I don't think my husband ever missed a day of work," says Charlotte.

During their years running the dairy, Charlotte and Speck rarely went on a vacation. Perhaps it was because Speck saw all of the world he cared to see during the war. Or, as Charlotte reflects, "He loved his work, and if he had it all to do over again, he'd probably do the same thing."

Speck died in 1992 at the age of 73. Now, at 86, Charlotte lives adjacent to the family farmhouse where she enjoys gardening and leads an active life.

12" x 12" finished

Materials:

- **Blue** (2½" x 20½")
- **Gold** (2½" x 12½")
- **Red** (⅛ yard)
- **Dark red** (3" x 12")
- **Beige** (⅛ yard)

Cutting Instructions:

 Cut 10 – 2" x 2"

 Cut 6 – 2" x 2"

 Cut 2 – 2" x 18"

 Cut 4 – 2³/₈" x 2³/₈"
Cut once diagonally.

 Cut 8 – 2" x 2"
Cut 8 – 2" x 3½"

 Cut 1 – 4¼" x 4¼"
Cut twice diagonally.
Triangles for Y-seams.

Cutting Instructions for Parallelograms:

From one red strip cut four 3¾" wide parallelograms at a 45° angle. Repeat with remaining red strip, reversing the direction of the cuts. See diagram.

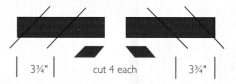

3¾"   cut 4 each   3¾"

Please refer to General Directions, page 13, for Y–Seams used in this block.

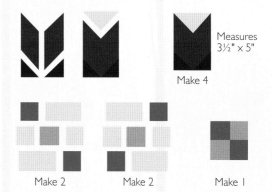

Measures 3½" x 5"

Make 4

Make 2   Make 2   Make 1

Block Construction:

1. Sew Row 1, as shown.
2. Sew Row 2, as shown.
3. Sew Row 3, as shown.
4. Press seams in direction of ⇄.
5. Sew Rows 1, 2 & 3 together.
6. Press finished block.

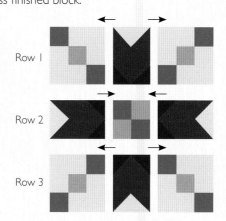

Row 1

Row 2

Row 3

Dan and Lisa Sheller
Eldora, Iowa

About 10 years ago, Lisa Powell, a single woman living in Iowa City, Iowa, logged on to Country Connections, an online dating service committed to matching compatible men and women who live in rural areas. Her first "connection" with a man from New Jersey didn't work, but that didn't discourage her; she tried again. Making her second electronic connection, Lisa learned she was corresponding with a man from Iowa by a comment he made about that state's Amana Colonies. Lisa and Dan Sheller met, discovered many common interests and values, and fell in love.

Photography (above) Copyright 2005 Ruth Ratliff

After dating and living together for a couple months, Lisa proposed to Dan. (She admits to being a "modern woman.") Dan, confessing that he wasn't quite ready to take the plunge, told Lisa that he thought they should wait a little while. Five years later, in the car on the way to a bicycle trail ride in Omaha, Dan said, "What do you think, should we get married?" And so they did, on July 8, 2000.

Lisa Sheller wishes she could be a quilt maker like her grandmother and great-grandmother, but she lacks the patience it takes to "cut fabric into a million little pieces and then sew it together again." Worried and disappointed that she wouldn't have a special treasure, like the quilt her Grandma Margaret gave her, to hand down someday, Lisa decided on a barn quilt instead. Because the farm's barn had collapsed several years prior, she had the quilt block painted directly on the antique corn crib instead. The historic barn isn't completely out of the picture, though, because Lisa reconstructed its old doors and uses them as a framework in her peony garden. This idea, she acknowledges, wasn't totally hers; she got it from Martha Stewart.

Dan and Lisa Sheller live and farm in the community where Dan grew up. Farms are getting bigger—"going corporate," Dan says. Farm family descendants are moving into cities for higher education and jobs. A rural guy through and through, Dan proudly admits, "You can't take farming out of me."

12" × 12" finished

Materials:

✛ **Plum** (¼ yard)
✛ **Green** (¼ yard)
✛ **Blue** (¼ yard)

Cutting Instructions:

 Cut 1 – 6⁷⁄₈" × 6⁷⁄₈"
Cut once diagonally.

Cut 1 – 5¹⁄₈" × 5¹⁄₈"
Cut once diagonally.

Cut 1 – 3⁷⁄₈" × 3⁷⁄₈"
Cut once diagonally.

 Cut 2 – 2⁵⁄₈" × 2⁵⁄₈"

 Cut 1 – 6⁷⁄₈" × 6⁷⁄₈"
Cut once diagonally.
Only one triangle used.

Cut 1 – 5¹⁄₈" × 5¹⁄₈"
Cut once diagonally.
Only one triangle used.

Cut 1 – 3⁷⁄₈" × 3⁷⁄₈"
Cut once diagonally.
Only one triangle used.

 Cut 1 – 2⁵⁄₈" × 2⁵⁄₈"

 Cut 1 – 6⁷⁄₈" × 6⁷⁄₈"
Cut once diagonally.
Only one triangle used.

Cut 1 – 5¹⁄₈" × 5¹⁄₈"
Cut once diagonally.
Only one triangle used.

Cut 1 – 3⁷⁄₈" × 3⁷⁄₈"
Cut once diagonally.
Only one triangle used.

 Cut 1 – 2⁵⁄₈" × 2⁵⁄₈"

Please refer to General Directions, page 13, for Square in a Square used in steps 2, 3 & 4 in this block.

Block Construction:

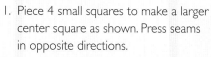

1. Piece 4 small squares to make a larger center square as shown. Press seams in opposite directions.
2. Sew 4 small triangles to center square, as shown. Press seams outward.
3. Add 4 medium triangles, as shown. Press seams outward.
4. Add 4 large triangles, as shown. Press seams outward.
5. Press finished block.

Horace and Doris Adams
Humboldt, Iowa

Two years after Horace and Doris Adams married in 1947, they designed and built a 32' X 60' barn on property that Horace's grandfather homesteaded in 1869. When the barn was completed, a Sunday school class from the Methodist Church asked to use it for a square dance. Young people danced to a caller and songs played by a fiddler late into the night. Hay bales served as furniture. Soon after, a second group asked if they, too, could have a dance in the barn; they knew once the cows were moved in, from then on the barn would be used for its intended purpose, which was not dancing.

Doris didn't grow up on a farm. After she married Horace, she received on-the-job training, such as learning to drive tractor. After tangling in the fence just once, she didn't do much more farm work for Horace and concentrated instead on raising their five children.

Back then, a corn crop might yield 30 to 60 bushels per acre. Today, yields may top 175 to 200 bushels per acre. Times were different then. Planting was done with a horse-drawn, two-row planter—not computer driven tractors with air-conditioning and built-in coffeemakers. When asked how to keep corn rows straight when planting with a horse and plow, Horace replies, "Get up sober!"

Neighbors were neighbors in those days, too. "It was second nature to help families on neighboring farms when they needed it," Doris remembers. An emergency appendectomy for Horace one summer brought neighbors from far and wide to help cultivate. It's the way it was back then.

Horace, an avid antique car enthusiast and long-time member of Humboldt Model A Club, is the proud owner of two classic cars—a Woody and a 1928 Model A Ford.

Horace, age 96, and Doris, age 87, live in a senior apartment complex in town now. Horace enjoys surfing the net and keeping up with friends and relatives on Facebook, while Doris works jigsaw puzzles and plays cards with neighbors.

Doris selected their barn quilt pattern by its name, Corn and Beans. The block was painted by a local 4-H group and installed by Rural Electrical Cooperative. She and Horace were delighted when they saw it was painted in green and yellow, traditional John Deere colors.

BIG SUNDAY SCHOOL PARTY.....
JUNE 28th, 8:15 P.M. at the
HORACE ADAMS' new barn......
6 miles west and 2-1/2 miles
south of Junction Highways
3 and 169.

COME IN JEANS!! The stairway goes straight up. Heap big fun!! DON'T MISS IT........
WE WANT A BIG CROWD...We are figuring on YOU.

FUN!   OLD TIME MUSIC!   LUNCH TOO!

cd   Home Builders Class Committee.

THIS SIDE OF CARD IS FOR ADDRESS

Mr. & Mrs. Horace Adams
Gilmore City, Iowa

12" x 12" finished

Materials:

- ✤ **Beige** (¼ yard)
- ✤ **2 Greens** (3" x 6")
- ✤ **2 Golds** (3" x 6")
- ✤ **4 medium florals** (5" x 5")
- ✤ **4 large florals** (5" x 5")

Cutting Instructions:

Background:

Cut 2 – 4⁷/₈" x 4⁷/₈"
Cut once diagonally.
Cut 10 – 2⁷/₈" x 2⁷/₈"
Cut once diagonally.

Small triangles:

Cut 2 – 2⁷/₈" x 2⁷/₈"
Cut once diagonally.

Cut 2 – 2⁷/₈" x 2⁷/₈"
Cut once diagonally.

Cut 2 – 2⁷/₈" x 2⁷/₈"
Cut once diagonally.

Cut 2 – 2⁷/₈" x 2⁷/₈"
Cut once diagonally.

Medium triangles:

Cut 1 – 3¾" x 3¾"
Cut once diagonally.

Cut 1 – 3¾" x 3¾"
Cut once diagonally.

Cut 1 – 3¾" x 3¾"
Cut once diagonally.

Cut 1 – 3¾" x 3¾"
Cut once diagonally.

Large triangles:

Cut 1 – 4⁷/₈" x 4⁷/₈"
Cut once diagonally.

Cut 1 – 4⁷/₈" x 4⁷/₈"
Cut once diagonally.

Cut 1 – 4⁷/₈" x 4⁷/₈"
Cut once diagonally.

Cut 1 – 4⁷/₈" x 4⁷/₈"
Cut once diagonally.

IMPORTANT NOTE:
All of the pieces in this block are cut on the bias. Please take care not to stretch.

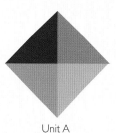

Unit A

There will be unused triangles when you are finished constructing the block.

Unit B – Make one of each color combination.

Unit C – Make one of each color combination.

Block Construction:

1. Sew one Unit B to each side of Unit A. Press outward.
2. Sew one medium triangle to each side. Press outward.
3. Sew one Unit C to each corner of block matching the colors from Units B. Press outward.

Jim and Jean Turner
Arlington, Iowa

Jim Turner, a retired Air Force colonel who relocated 11 times during his distinguished military career, said, "If the windows in the house were dirty, it was time to move again." During 28 years of service, Jim logged over 8,000 air hours in planes he flew such as B52's and FB111's, which sometimes carried nuclear weapons. "I joined the Air Force because I wasn't about to walk the war," Jim says. Humbly, he adds, "I'm just thankful that my take-offs equaled my landings."

Jim and his wife Jean are back home now, living in Arlington, Iowa, on property adjacent to land that Jim's grandfather homesteaded in 1852 when he arrived in the United States. Eventually, his grandfather divided his estate into farms—one 120 acres for each of his 17 children (except for one son, a stallion breeder, who received 60 acres instead).

The historic barn is supported by enormous wooden beams that were floated down the Mississippi River from Wisconsin to Clayton, Iowa, where they were then hauled by oxen about 40 miles to the farm. Sand dug from the Volga River, about eight miles from Arlington, was lugged to the farm by an ox team and used to make concrete. Over 1,000 hand-hewn wooden pegs were used to hold the barn together. "Remarkably, there was not a single metal nail in the entire barn," Jim says. In 1910, after the barn and other farm buildings were complete, his grandfather built the family's house.

Jim grew up milking cows on his parents' dairy farm. To be absolutely, positively certain that he would never ever have to milk another cow, Jim has converted the antique barn into a party barn that he and Jean rent out for all sorts of celebratory events.

Jean learned about the barn quilts from a friend who asked if she might be interested in hanging one on their barn. From a list of available quilt blocks provided by the Fayette County Barn Quilt office, Jean selected her three favorite quilt blocks, which she then hand-colored on paper samples to be sure she would get a bright one. She was pleased with the Card Trick block because it reminded her of Jim's mother, who loved to play cards. The block was painted in bright colors that she liked.

12" × 12" finished

Materials:

❖ **Red** (6" × 12")
❖ **Gold** (6" × 12")
❖ **Blue** (6" × 12")
❖ **Green** (6" × 12")
❖ **Charcoal** (12" × 12")

Cutting Instructions:

Cut 1 – 4⅞" × 4⅞"
Cut once diagonally. Use for large triangles.

Cut 1 – 5¼" × 5¼"
Cut twice diagonally. Use for small triangles.
(2 triangles will not be used)

Cut 1 – 4⅞" × 4⅞"
Cut once diagonally. Use for large triangles.

Cut 1 – 5¼" × 5¼"
Cut twice diagonally. Use for small triangles.
(2 triangles will not be used)

Cut 1 – 4⅞" × 4⅞"
Cut once diagonally. Use for large triangles.

Cut 1 – 5¼" × 5¼"
Cut twice diagonally. Use for small triangles.
(2 triangles will not be used)

Cut 1 – 4⅞" × 4⅞"
Cut once diagonally. Use for large triangles.

Cut 1 – 5¼" × 5¼"
Cut twice diagonally. Use for small triangles.
(2 triangles will not be used)

Cut 2 – 4⅞" × 4⅞"
Cut once diagonally. Use for large triangles.

Cut 1 – 5¼" × 5¼"
Cut twice diagonally. Use for small triangles.
(You will use all 4 triangles.)

Please refer to General Directions, page 13, for half square triangles, used in this block.

Center – make 1.

Make 1 of each color combination.
Press toward charcoal triangle.

Make 1 of each color combination. Press toward large triangle.

Block Construction:

1. Row 1 – Sew together, as shown.
2. Row 2 – Sew together, as shown.
3. Row 3 – Sew together, as shown.
4. Press seams in direction of ⇄.
5. Sew Rows 1, 2 & 3 together.
6. Press finished block.

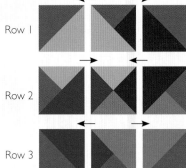

Row 1
Row 2
Row 3

Marv and Marlys Haverkamp
Grundy Center, Iowa

Growing up in Nebraska during the Depression wasn't easy for the Haverkamp family. "But you know what," Marv Haverkamp says, "somehow we always managed to have something to eat. I don't know how that happened, but we always ate."

Times were especially tough for farmers during the Depression. From 1930 to 1936, drought destroyed crops and parched farm land. Then strong sustained winds turned the soil to dust. With no plantings to keep the earth in place, large black clouds formed, often reducing visibility to just a few feet. Dust blew as far as New York City and Washington D.C., ultimately depositing the dirt in the Atlantic Ocean. These harsh years became known as the Dirty Thirties and the Dust Bowl.

Marv received his education in a one-room country school. Each student had daily chores at school, such as pumping water and hauling firewood, in addition to their farm chores. When chores at school were done, education began.

One day when a schoolyard snowball fight began, Marv sought refuge in the schoolhouse. He pulled on the door handle, only to have the knob fall off in his hand. Although it had been an innocent act, word of Marv's dirty deed traveled quickly to his home where Marv says he "met the board of education," which he exemplified by rubbing his backside.

In 1940, Marv's parents and their eight children relocated to Sumner, Iowa, where Marv married Marlys and farmed for 18 years. Later he worked at a fertilizer plant in Grundy Center, Iowa, before commencing a 30-year career as an over-the-road truck driver. Marv and Marlys adopted and raised five children.

Marv has chosen principles of "common sense and integrity over power and greed" to guide him through his 84 years. He begins every day by saying, "Thanks, Lord, for helping me."

12" × 12" finished

Materials:

✤ **Green** (1/8 yard)
  Cream (1/8 yard)
✤ **Light Green** (1/8 yard)
✤ **Red** (1/8 yard)

Cutting Instructions:

 Cut 1 – 2½" × 2½"

 Cut 2 – 3⅞" × 3⅞"
Cut once diagonally.

 Cut 4 – 2½" × 2½"
 Cut 4 – 2½" × 5½"

 Cut 2 – 4¼" × 4¼"
Cut twice diagonally.

 Cut 2 – 2" × 14"

 Cut 2 – 2" × 14"

Cutting Instructions for Parallelograms:

- From light green strips cut **4** (total of 8) parallelogram units of each direction at a 45° angle.

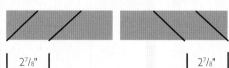

2⅞"   2⅞"

- From red strips cut **4** (total of 8) parallelogram units of each direction at a 45° angle.

2⅞"   2⅞"

Please refer to General Directions, page 13, for Y–Seams, used in this block.

Block Construction:

1. Row 1 – Sew together, as shown.
2. Row 2 – Sew together, as shown.
3. Row 3 – Sew together, as shown.
4. Press seams in direction of ⇄.
5. Sew Rows 1, 2 & 3 together.
6. Press finished block.

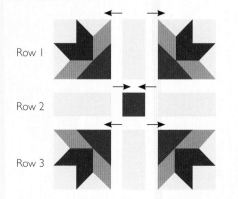

Row 1

Row 2

Row 3

Ann Zemke
Blaine, Minnesota

Every year without fail, the Zemke family of Red Wing, Minnesota, takes part in a Christmas caroling custom that now spans over half a century.

This Christmas Eve caroling extravaganza began out of necessity, when Ted and Mildred Zemke gathered their five daughters and two sons and their families to celebrate the holiday in 1955. After the customary buffet dinner, a houseful of sated adults and restless children knew it would soon be time to gather in the living room to open gifts. One rule, however, was always strictly enforced: NO gifts could be opened until the dishes were cleaned and put away.

Of course, it was almost impossible to contain the over-enthusiastic children who were eager to unwrap the special gift that had been selected for them by a cousin, aunt or uncle. So, on that fateful Christmas Eve of 1955, while the dishes were being washed, Uncle Cal offered to take the children caroling. This aided the digestion of a super-sized meal, helped the children pass time while temporarily keeping their minds off gift giving, and entertained (we hope) unwary neighbors.

More than 50 years have passed. The cast has changed but the holiday tradition lives on, and there's no end in sight!

12" × 12" finished

Materials:

- ❖ **Red** (5" × 5" scrap)
- ❖ **Green** (4" × 8" scrap)
- ❖ **Gold** (¹/₈ yard)
- ❖ **Tan** (¹/₈ yard)

Cutting Instructions:

 Cut 1 – 4¾" × 4¾"

 Cut 2 – 3⁷/₈" × 3⁷/₈"
Cut once diagonally.
Use for Square in a Square.

 Cut 8 – 3½" × 3½"
Use for Flying Geese.

 Cut 4 – 3½" × 3½"
Cut 4 – 3½" × 6½"

Please refer to General Directions, page 13, for Flying Geese and Square in a Square, used in this block.

 Make 4   Make 1

Block Construction:

1. Row 1 – Sew a 3½" × 3½" square to each side of the Flying Geese.
2. Row 2 – Sew a Flying Geese unit to each side of the Square in a Square.
3. Row 3 – Sew a 3½" × 3½" square to each side of the Flying Geese.
4. Press seams in direction of ⇄ .
5. Sew rows 1, 2 & 3 together.
6. Press finished block.

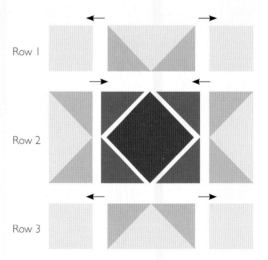

Row 1

Row 2

Row 3

The year was 1912. Pine Creek near Taylor, Wisconsin, held a sweet little farm where my grandmother grew up. She had a pet dog named Bobby, quite an extraordinary animal who loved to help out around the farm. One of his jobs was to round up the cows at milking times, and another was to help fill the wood box when it was empty. Great-Grandma Brager had him bring the wood in, one stick at a time.

Great-Grandma herself had a big job: to keep the home and gardens running while the men were out working the fields and tending to the animals. She also had to keep the men fed while they worked. To save her the time of walking all the way out to the far fields, Great-Grandma would strap the men's lunch bucket to Bobby's neck and give him pail of coffee to carry in his mouth.

One day when the dog didn't show up with their noon meal, the men made their way back to the farmhouse, assuming Great-Grandma had forgotten to send Bobby with the provisions. As it was, they discovered he had fallen into the creek and lost the lunch bucket in the water. But ever true to his nature, Bobby still held onto that coffee pail while trying to rescue the lunch.

On the farm, after work comes play—and Bobby was no exception. He was an excellent outfielder when the kids played ball. His days as an outfielder ended when some wise guy threw him a rock instead of the ball.

But that wasn't the end of Bobby, who got to be pretty old before he died. Generations later, we still remember his ability to work hard and his heroic efforts to save the farmhands' lunch.

Sister's Choice

12" x 12" finished

Materials:

+ **Red** (¹/₈ yard)
+ **Tan** (¹/₈ yard)
+ **Light Green** (¹/₈ yard)
+ **Dark Green** (¹/₈ yard)
+ **Gold** (¹/₈ yard)

Cutting Instructions:

 Cut 4 – 2⁷/₈" x 2⁷/₈"

 Cut 5 – 2⁷/₈" x 2⁷/₈"

 Cut 4 – 2⁷/₈" x 2⁷/₈"

 Cut 4 – 2⁷/₈" x 2⁷/₈"
 Cut 4 – 3 ¼" x 3¼"
Use for half square triangles.

 Cut 4 – 3¼" x 3¼"
Use for half square triangles.

Please refer to General Directions, page 13, for half square triangles used in this block.

 Make 8

Block Construction:

1. Row 1 – Sew together, as shown.
2. Row 2 – Sew together, as shown.
3. Row 3 – Sew together, as shown.
4. Row 4 – Sew together, as shown.
5. Row 5 – Sew together, as shown.
6. Press seams in direction of ⇄.
7. Sew rows 1, 2, 3, 4 & 5 together.
8. Press finished block.

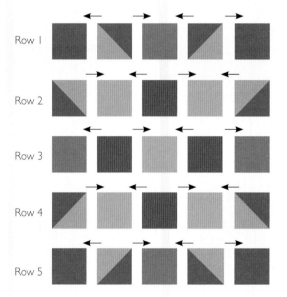

Row 1

Row 2

Row 3

Row 4

Row 5

*Photography Copyright 2009
Ruth Ratliff*

12" × 12" finished

Materials:

- ❖ **Dark Green** (4" × 13")
- ❖ **Medium Green** (4" × 10")
- ❖ **Light Green** (4" × 7")
- ❖ **Dark Gold** (4" × 12")
- ❖ **Medium Gold** (4" × 9")
- ❖ **Light Gold** (4" × 6")
- ❖ **Red** (4" × 4")

Cutting Instructions:

Cut 1 – 2" × 12½"
Cut 1 – 2" × 11"

Cut 1 – 2" × 9½"
Cut 1 – 2" × 8"

Cut 1 – 2" × 6½"
Cut 1 – 2" × 5"

Cut 1 – 2" × 11"
Cut 1 – 2" × 9½"

Cut 1 – 2" × 8"
Cut 1 – 2" × 6½"

Cut 1 – 2" × 5"
Cut 1 – 2" × 3½"

Cut 1 – 3½" × 3½"

Block Construction:

Lay out all pieces in order, as shown. Beginning from center block, attach strips in numerical order.

Press outward after attaching each strip.

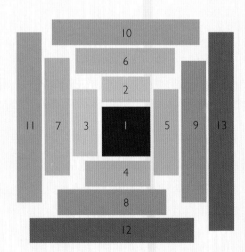

12" x 12" finished

Materials:

❖ **Brown** (¼ yard)
❖ **Tan** (¼ yard)

Cutting Instructions:

Cut 4 – $3^{15}/_{16}$" x $3^{15}/_{16}$"
Cut 1 – $2^{3}/_{16}$" x $2^{3}/_{16}$"
Cut 8 – $2^{9}/_{16}$" x $2^{9}/_{16}$"
Use for half square triangles.

Cut 4 – $2^{3}/_{16}$" x $2^{3}/_{16}$"
Cut 4 – $2^{3}/_{16}$" x $5^{5}/_{8}$"
Cut 8 – $2^{9}/_{16}$" x $2^{9}/_{16}$"
Use for half square triangles.

Please refer to General Directions, page 13, for half square triangles, used in this block.

Make 16

Block Construction:

1. Row 1 – Sew together, as shown.
2. Row 2 – Sew together, as shown.
3. Row 3 – Sew together, as shown.
4. Press seams in direction of ⇄ .
5. Sew Rows 1, 2 & 3 together.
6. Press finished block.

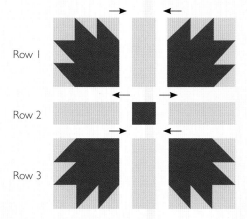

Row 1

Row 2

Row 3

12" × 12" finished

Materials:

❖ **Green** (¼ yard)
❖ **Gold** (¼ yard)

Cutting Instructions:

 Cut 1 – 3⅝" × 16"
Cut 1 – 7⅜" × 9"

 Cut 1 – 3⅞" × 3⅞"
Cut once diagonally.

 Cut 1 – 3⅝" × 16"
Cut 1 – 7⅜" × 9"

 Cut 1 – 3⅞" × 3⅞"
Cut once diagonally.

Block Construction:

1. Sew one accent triangle on each side of canoe triangle, as shown.
2. Add small triangle to the end of canoe triangle, as shown.
3. Make 2 of each color combination.

Blocks measure 6½" x 6½".

4. Press seams in direction of ⇄ .
5. Sew rows 1 & 2 together.
6. Press finished block.

Cutting Instructions for:

Accent triangles

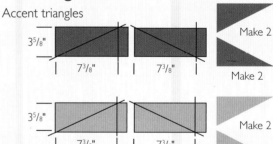

Canoe triangles

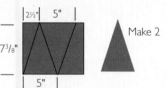

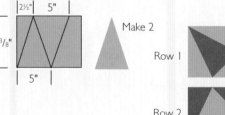

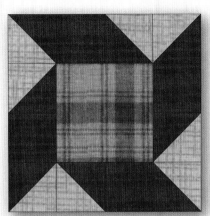

12" × 12" finished

Photography Copyright 2007 Ruth Ratliff

Materials:

❖ **Plaid** (6½" × 6½")
❖ **Red** (⅛ yard)
❖ **Beige** (⅛ yard)

Cutting Instructions:

 Cut 1 – 6½" × 6½"

 Cut 4 – 3½" × 3½"
Cut 4 – 3⅞" × 3⅞"
Use for half square triangles.

 Cut 4 – 3⅞" × 3⅞"
Use for half square triangles.

Please refer to General Directions, page 13, for half square triangles used in this block.

 Make 8

Block Construction:

1. Row 1 – Sew together, as shown.
2. Row 2:
   • Sew one half square triangle and one square together, as shown.
   • Sew one of these units to each side of center square, as shown.
3. Row 3 – Sew together, as shown.
4. Press seams in direction of ⇄.
5. Sew Rows 1, 2 & 3 together.
6. Press finished block.

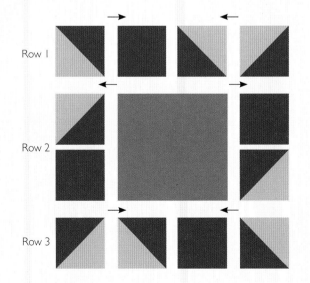

Row 1

Row 2

Row 3

*Photography Copyright 2009
Ruth Ratliff*

12" x 12" finished

Materials:

- **Taupe** (¹/₈ yard)
- **Rust** (¹/₈ yard)
- **Light Tan** (¹/₈ yard)
- **Green** (¹/₈ yard)
- **Dark Tan** (¹/₈ yard)

Cutting Instructions:

Cut 2 – 1½" x 2½"
Cut 2 – 1½" x 4½"
Cut 2 – 1¹⁵/₁₆" x 6³/₁₆"
Cut 2 – 1¹⁵/₁₆" x 9"

Cut 1 – 1¹⁵/₁₆" x 1¹⁵/₁₆"
Center square.
Cut 4 – 2⁷/₈" x 2⁷/₈"
Use for larger half square triangles.

Cut 2 – 1⁷/₈" x 1⁷/₈"
Cut once diagonally.
Use for Square in a Square.

Cut 6 – 2⁷/₈" x 2⁷/₈"
Use for larger half square triangles.

Cut 6 – 2⁷/₈" x 2⁷/₈"
Cut once diagonally.

Cut 2 – 2⁷/₈" x 2⁷/₈"
Use for larger half square triangles.
Cut 2 – 2³/₁₆" x 2³/₁₆"
Use for smaller half square triangles.

Cut 2 – 2³/₁₆" x 2³/₁₆"
Use for smaller half square triangles.

Cut 2 – 3³/₁₆" x 3³/₁₆"
Cut twice diagonally.

Please refer to General Directions page 13, for half square triangles and Square in a Square, used in this block.

 Make 4   Make 4   Make 8 Make 4

A Unit

 Make 4

B Unit

Block Construction:
After each step, press seam outward.

1. Make a Square in a Square.

2. Sew a 1½" x 2½" strip on each side of Square in a Square.

3. Sew a 1½" x 4½" strip on opposite sides of Square in a Square.

4. Add four A Units to the sides of Step 2 unit.

5. Sew two 1¹⁵/₁₆" x 6³/₁₆" strips to opposite sides of Step 3 unit.

6. Sew a 1¹⁵/₁₆" x 9" strip on remaining sides of unit.

7. Add four B Units to corners, as shown.

8. Press finished block.

12" x 12" finished

Materials:

❖ **Rust** (1/8 yard)
❖ **Green** (1/8 yard)
❖ **Gold** (1/4 yard)

Cutting Instructions:

 Cut 1 – 3" x 30"

 Cut 1 – 3" x 30"

 Cut 1 – 6¼" x 6¼"
Cut twice diagonally.

 Cut 4 – 4" x 4"

Cutting Instructions for Star Points:

• From green strips, cut 4 diamond shapes at a 45° angle.

| 4¼" |

• From rust strips, cut 4 diamond shapes at a 45° angle.

| 4¼" |

Block Construction:

1. Sew four pairs of rust/green star points together. Sew gold triangle to "V" of star points, referring to Y–Seam Directions, page 13.

2. Sew gold square to green edge of above unit.

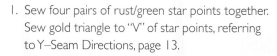

Make 4

3. Sew two of above units together, as shown, referring to Y-Seam directions.

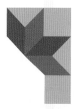

Make 2

4. Sew two above units together to form star, as shown, referring to Y-Seam directions.

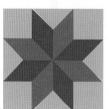

5. Press finished block.

Dutchman's Puzzle

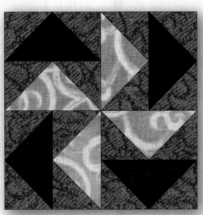

12" × 12" finished

Materials:

❖ **Gold** (¹/₈ yard)
❖ **Black** (¹/₈ yard)
❖ **Green** (¼ yard)

Cutting Instructions:

 Cut 4 – 3½" × 6½"

 Cut 4 – 3½" × 6½"

 Cut 16 – 3½" × 3½"

Please refer to General Directions, page 13, for Flying Geese, used in this block.

Make 4   Make 4

Block Construction:

1. Sew one of each color combination together to make one unit, as shown.

2. Sew two units together, as shown, to make Row 1 and Row 2.

 Make 4

3. Press seams in direction of ⇄.

4. Sew rows 1 & 2 together.

5. Press finished block.

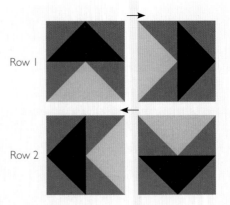

Row 1

Row 2

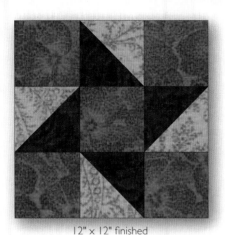

12" × 12" finished

Materials:

- **Blue** (¼ yard)
- **Red** (¼ yard)
- **Gold** (¼ yard)

Cutting Instructions:

 Cut 5 – 4½" × 4½"

 Cut 2 – 4⅞" × 4⅞"
Use for half square triangles.

 Cut 2 – 4⅞" × 4⅞"
Use for half square triangles.

Please refer to General Directions, page 13, for half square triangles, used in this block.

 Make 4

Block Construction:

1. Row 1 – Sew together, as shown.
2. Row 2 – Sew together, as shown.
3. Row 3 – Sew together, as shown.
4. Press seams in direction of ⇄.
5. Sew rows 1, 2 & 3 together.
6. Press finished block.

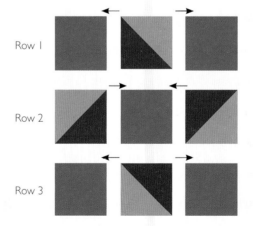

Row 1

Row 2

Row 3

Contrary Wife

12" × 12" finished

Materials:

- ❖ **Red** (5" × 10")
- ❖ **Gold** (5" × 15")
- ❖ **Green** (5" × 12")
- ❖ **Tan** (5" × 12")

Cutting Instructions:

 Cut 2 – 4½" × 4½"

 Cut 3 – 4½" x4½"

 Cut 2 – 5" × 5"
Use for half square triangles.

 Cut 2 – 5" × 5"
Use for half square triangles.

Please refer to General Directions, page 13, for half square triangles used in this block.

 Make 4

Block Construction:

1. Row 1 – Sew together, as shown.
2. Row 2 – Sew together, as shown.
3. Row 3 – Sew together, as shown.
4. Press seams in direction of ⇄.
5. Sew Rows 1, 2 & 3 together.
6. Press finished block.

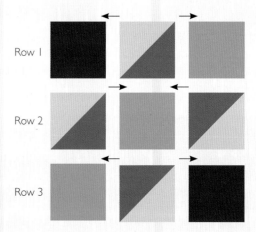

The Contrary Wife quilt block displayed on the Fettkether barn (page 14) is an example of a quilt block variation and used to sew the Contrary Wife block in the Barn Dance sampler quilt.

Quilts &
Other Projects

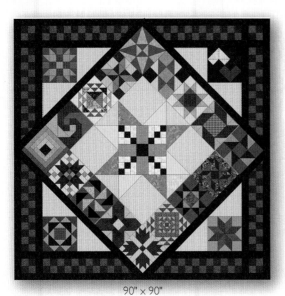

90" x 90"

Materials to Complete Quilt:

❖ **Red** – 1 yard
Checkerboard border.

❖ **Orange** – 1 yard
Checkerboard border.

Tan – ⅝ yard
Background for corner units.

❖ **Dark Brown** – 2¾ yards
Dark borders.

Center Quilt Construction:

Step 1 – Sew Center Block together. Refer to directions, page 53.

Step 2 – Sew 2 units of 3 blocks together, as shown. Sew these units to opposite sides of center block.

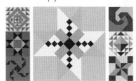

Step 3 – Sew 2 units of 5 blocks together, as shown. Sew these units to opposite sides of center block.

Checkerboard Border:

• Cut 10 strips (orange) 3" x WOF.
• Cut 10 strips (red) 3" x WOF.

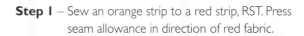

Step 1 – Sew an orange strip to a red strip, RST. Press seam allowance in direction of red fabric.

Step 2 – Cut 120 units 3" x 5 ½".

Step 3 – Sew pairs of Step 2 units together, alternating the two colors, as shown.

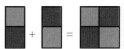

Unit A – make 60

Unit A measures 5½" x 5½"

Step 4 – Use 56 of 4-patch units from Step 3 to make Unit B below.
• Sew seven 4-patch units together, as shown.
• Make 8.

Unit B

Set aside remaining four 4-patch units for the corners.

From Dark Borders Cut:

Strip A - Cut 4 strips 3" × 33"
Strip B - Cut 4 strips 3" × 5½"
Strip C - Cut 4 strips 3" × 38"
Strip D - Cut 4 strips 3" × 64½"

From Tan Cut:

Cut 2 – 18¼" × 18¼"
Cut twice diagonally.

Corner Construction:

Step 1 – Sew short edge of triangle to one edge of pieced block. Sew 2nd triangle to adjacent edge of pieced block. Refer to diagram. Press toward triangles.

Step 2 – Sew one Strip A to one of the checkerboard units. Press toward Strip A.

Step 3 – Sew checkerboard/Strip A unit to pieced block/triangle unit. Press toward Strip A.

Step 4 – Sew a 4-patch, a Strip B and a checkerboard unit together. Refer to diagram. Press toward Strip B.

Step 5 – Sew 1 Strip C to Step 4 unit. Press toward Strip C.

Step 6 – Sew this unit to unit created in Step 3. Press toward Strip C.

Step 7 – Trim extensions of Strip/checkerboard units. Fig. 1.

Step 8 – Sew Strip D to long edge of corner unit. Press toward strip. Fig. 1a.

Step 9 – Trim extensions. Fig. 2.

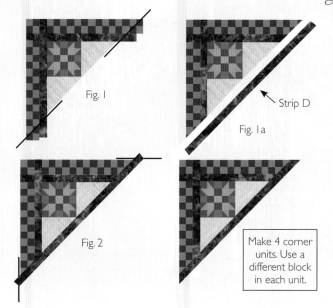

Fig. 1

Fig. 1a

Strip D

Fig. 2

Make 4 corner units. Use a different block in each unit.

Sew 4 corner units, centering on each side of center unit, as shown.

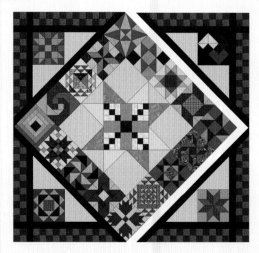

Outer Borders:

Cut 2 strips 3" × 85"
• Sew these strips to each side of quilt.
Cut 2 strips 3" × 90"
• Sew these strips to top and bottom of quilt.

Finishing:

• Layer and quilt, using your favorite method.
• Binding. Cut 9 strips 2½" × WOF. Sew strips together, press wrong sides together, lengthwise.

CENTER BLOCK

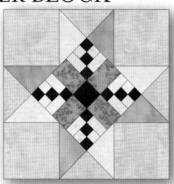

36" × 36" finished

Materials:

- ❖ **Dark Red** (¼ yard)
- ❖ **Gold** (¼ yard)
- ❖ **Cream** (⅛ yard)
- ❖ **Orange** (½ yard)
- ❖ **Yellow** (½ yard)
- ❖ **Beige** (¾ yard)

Cutting Instructions:

Center Section:

 Cut 12 – 2⅝" × 2⅝"
Cut 1 – 4¾" × 4¾"
Use for chain block.

 Cut 4 – 4¾" × 6⅞"

 Cut 8 – 2⅝" × 2⅝"
Cut 8 – 2⅝" × 4¾"
Use for chain block.

Star Points and Background:

 Cut 1 – 13¼" × 13¼"
Cut twice diagonally.

 Cut 1 – 13¼" × 13¼"
Cut twice diagonally.

 Cut 4 – 12½" × 12½"

 Cut 1 – 13¼" × 13¼"
Cut twice diagonally.

Chain Block Construction:

1. Sew four 2⅝" × 2⅝" squares together, as shown. Press toward red squares.

2. Sew a 2⅝" × 4¾" rectangle to side of a four-patch unit. Press toward four-patch.

3. Sew a 2⅝" red square to a 2⅝" × 4¾" cream rectangle. Press toward red square.

4. Add rectangle unit to four-patch unit.

5. Press completed nine-patch. Make 4.

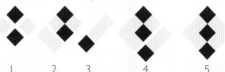

1.   2.   3.   4.   5.

Center Section Construction:

1. Row 1 – Sew a nine-patch block to each side of a 4¾" × 6⅞" gold rectangle, as shown.

2. Row 2 – Sew together, as shown.

3. Row 3 – repeat instructions as in Row 1, as shown.

4. Press seams in direction of ⇄.

5. Sew Rows 1, 2 & 3 together.

6. Press finished block.

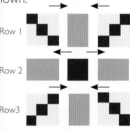

Row 1
Row 2
Row3
17½" × 17½"

Star Points Construction:

1. Unit A – Sew long edge of one orange triangle to beige square. Then sew one long edge of yellow triangle to adjacent side of square. Refer to diagram for color placement.

2. Unit B – Sew one beige triangle (short side) to each side of Unit A, as shown.

Make 4
Unit A

Make 2
Unit B

Center Block Construction:

1. Sew one Unit A to each side of Inner Block, as shown. Fig.1.

2. Sew one Unit B to each side of Inner Block, as shown. Fig.2.

3. Press finished block.

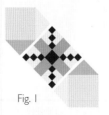

Fig. 1   Fig. 2

87½" × 87½"

Materials to Complete Quilt:

✤ **Green** – 2½ yard
Center unit, outer border and binding.

✤ **Brown** – 1¾ yards
Center unit, borders and sashing.

✤ **Tan** – ⅞ yard
Center Unit.

✤ **Gold** – ½ yard
Inner border.

Cutting Instructions for Center:

  Cut 8 – 2" × 9"
Cut 4 – 2" × 18½"

  Cut 8 – 2" × 9"
Cut 4 – 2" × 18½"

  Cut 4 – 9" × 9"
Cut 4 – 9" × 18½"

Center Unit Construction:

Step 1 – Construct the Goose Tracks block referring to
directions for an 18" × 18" finished block on page 57.

Step 2 – Sew green and brown 2" × 9" strips together.
RST Press toward brown strip.

Make 8 Units

Step 3 – Sew green and brown 2" × 18½" strips together.
RST Press toward brown strip.

Make 4 Units

Step 4 – Sew green and brown 2" × 16" strips together.
RST Press seam allowance in direction of brown
fabric.

| 2" | Make 1 Unit
Cut 8 Units

Make 4 - 4 Patch Units

Step 5 – Sew rows 1, 2, 3, 4 & 5, as shown.
Step 6 – Press in direction of ⇄ .
Step 7 – Sew rows together to complete center unit.
Step 8 – Press unit.

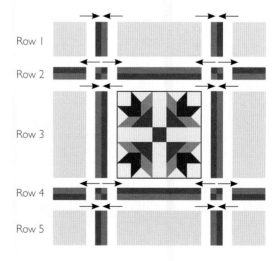

Row 1

Row 2

Row 3

Row 4

Row 5

Cutting Instructions for Sashing:

Cut 12 strips 3" x 12½"
Cut 2 strips 3" x 41½"
Cut 2 strips 3" x 70½"

Quilt Construction:

Step 1 – Sew a 3" x 41½" strip to each side of center block, as shown. Press towards strip.

Step 2 – Sew 2 units of 3 blocks together, as shown, sewing 3" x 12½" sashing strips between blocks. Press toward sashing strip.

Step 3 – Sew these units to 3" x 41½" strips sewn to sides of center block. Press toward sashing strips.

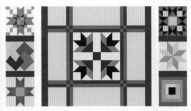

Step 4 – Sew a 3" x 70½" strip to top and bottom of unit, as shown. Press toward strip.

Step 5 – Sew two units of 5 blocks together, as shown, sewing 3" x 12½" strips between blocks. Press toward sashing strips.

Step 6 – Sew these units to the top and bottom of center unit, as shown. Press toward sashing strips.

Adding Borders:

Inner border (brown):
Sew a 2½" x 70½" strip to top and bottom of unit. Sew a 2½" x 74½" strip to each side of unit. Press toward borders.

Middle border (gold):
Sew a 2" x 74½" strip to top and bottom of unit. Press outward. Sew a 2" x 77½" strip to sides of unit. Press toward borders.

Outer border (green):
Sew a 5½" x 77½" strip to top and bottom of unit. Press outward. Sew a 5½" x 87½" strip to sides of unit. Press outward.

Finishing:

• Layer and quilt, using your favorite method.
• Binding. Cut 9 strips 2½" x WOF. Sew strips together, press wrong sides together, lengthwise.

CENTER BLOCK

18" × 18" finished

Materials:

- ✤ **Blue** 10" × 12"
- ✤ **Beige** ¼ yard
- ✤ **Green** ⅛ yard
- ✤ **Red** ⅛ yard

Cutting Instructions:

 Cut 1 – 3½" × 3½"

 Cut 2 – 5⅜" × 5⅜"
Cut once diagonally.

 Cut 4 – 3½" × 3½"
 Cut 4 – 3½" × 8"

 Cut 2 – 6⅛" × 6⅛"
Cut twice diagonally.

 Cut 2 – 2⅝" × 22"

 Cut 2 – 2⅝" × 22"

Cutting Instructions for Parallelograms:

- From green strips cut **4** (total of 8) parallelogram units of each direction at a 45° angle.

4⅛"   4⅛"

- From red strips cut **4** (total of 8) parallelogram units of each direction at a 45° angle.

4⅛"   4⅛"

Please refer to General Directions, page 13, for Y–Seams, used in this block.

Block Construction:

1. Row 1 – Sew together, as shown.
2. Row 2 – Sew together, as shown.
3. Row 3 – Sew together, as shown.
4. Press seams in direction of ⇄.
5. Sew Rows 1, 2, & 3 together.
6. Press finished block.

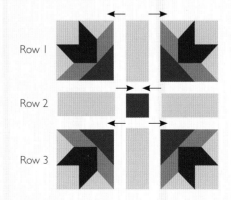

Row 1

Row 2

Row 3

35" × 35"

Materials:

- **Red** – ½ yard
- **Light green** – ¼ yard
- **Dark green** – ½ yard
- **Cream** – 1⅜ yard
- **Binding** – ⅓ yard
- **Backing** – 1⅛ yards

Fig. 1

Cutting Instructions for Borders and Corners:

 Cut 4 – 2" × 24½"

 Cut 4 – 2" × 24½"

 Cut 2 – 13⅞" × 13⅞"
Cut once diagonally.

Construction of Quilt:

1. Construct 4 Goose Track blocks (directions on page 35).
2. Sew 4 Goose Tracks blocks together as shown. Fig. 1.
3. Sew red and green strips together, RST. Press seam allowance in direction of green fabric.
4. Add one cream triangle to the green/red unit made in Step 2, be sure to center triangle. Make 4.
5. Center and sew on each of the 4 corner units from Step 3. Fig. 1.
6. Trim extensions of strip/Goose Tracks unit. Fig. 2. See trim line on Fig. 2.

> Be sure there is ¼" from cutting line to point of cream square.

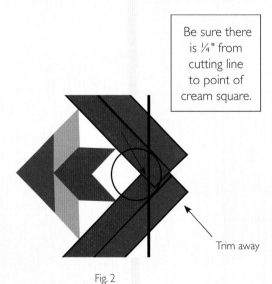

Trim away

Fig. 2

Finishing:

- Layer and quilt, using your favorite method.
- Binding. Cut 4 strips 2½" × WOF (dark green). Sew strips together, press wrong sides together, lengthwise.

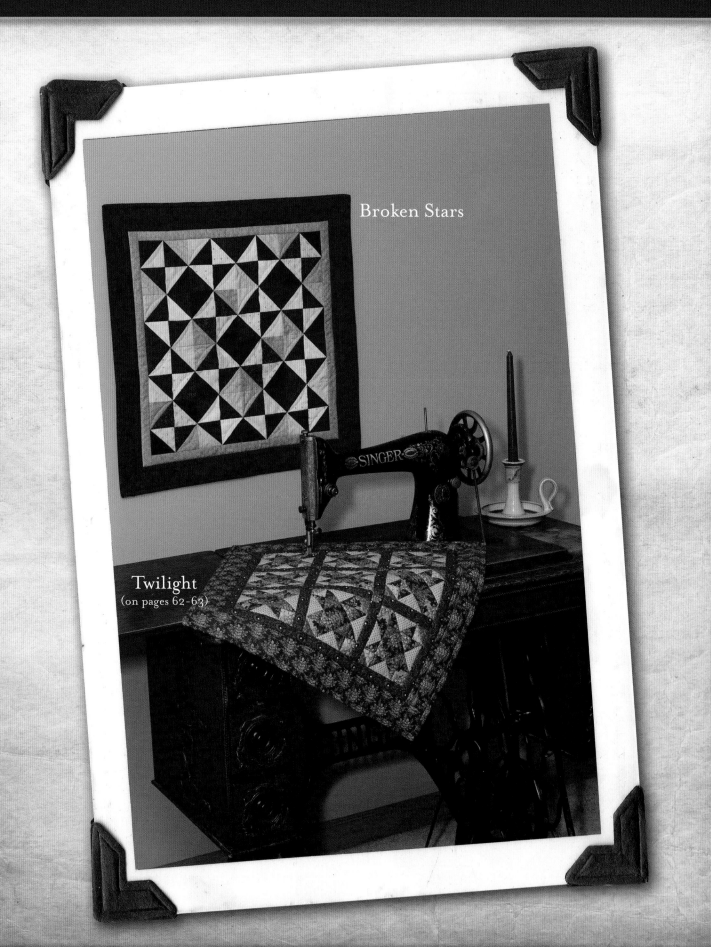

Broken Stars

Twilight
(on pages 62-63)

21" × 21"

Materials:

❖ **Reds** – I strip each of 8 different reds – $2^{7}/_{8}$" × $12\frac{1}{2}$". From each strip cut four $2^{7}/_{8}$" × $2^{7}/_{8}$" squares.

❖ **Beiges** – I strip of each beige – $2^{7}/_{8}$" × $12\frac{1}{2}$". From each strip cut four $2^{7}/_{8}$" × $2^{7}/_{8}$" squares.

❖ **Ist border (beige)** – $^{1}/_{8}$ yard

❖ **2nd border and binding (red)** – $\frac{1}{4}$ yard

Backing – ¾ yard

 Layer one red $2^{7}/_{8}$" × $12\frac{1}{2}$" strip with one beige $2^{7}/_{8}$" × $12\frac{1}{2}$" strip, RST. Repeat with remaining red and beige fabrics.
- Sub cut each pair into four $2^{7}/_{8}$" squares and proceed with half square triangle directions on page 13. Make 64 half square triangles.

Block Construction: 4" × 4" finished

 Each block consists of 2 different red/beige combinations. Refer to diagram for color placement.

Make 4 blocks of each red/beige combination.

Sew 4 rows of 4 blocks to construct quilt body.

Cutting Instructions and Border Construction for 1st, 2nd Borders:

Ist border:

Cut 2 strips – $1\frac{1}{4}$" × $16\frac{1}{2}$".
- Sew strips to top and bottom of constructed quilt, as shown. Fig. I.

Cut 2 strips – $1\frac{1}{4}$" × 18".
- Sew strips to remaining sides of quilt, as shown. Fig. I.

2nd border:

Cut 2 strips – $2\frac{1}{4}$" × 18".
- Sew strips to top and bottom of Ist border, as shown. Fig. I.

Cut 2 strips – $2\frac{1}{4}$" × 21".
- Sew strips to remaining sides of Ist border, as shown. Fig. I.

Fig. I

Finishing:

- Layer and quilt, using your favorite method.
- Binding. Cut 3 strips $2\frac{1}{4}$" × WOF. Sew strips together, press wrong sides together, lengthwise.

18½" x 18½"

Materials:

✤ **2 Light blues** – ⅛ yard each
✤ **Dark blue** – ⅜ yard
   For piecing, borders and binding.
✤ **Light brown** – ⅛ yard
✤ **Dark brown** – ¼ yard
   For piecing and sashing.
Backing – ⅝ yard

Please refer to General Directions, page 13, for half square triangle units, Square in a Square and Flying Geese, used in this quilt.

Cutting Instructions for Twilight block:

 Cut 18 – 1⅞" x 1⅞"
Use for ½ square triangles.

 Cut 9 – 1⅞" x 1⅞"
Use for ½ square triangles.

 Cut 9 – 1⅞" x 1⅞"
Use for ½ square triangles.

 Make 18 units of each color combination.

 Cut 9 – 1¹⁵/₁₆" x 1¹⁵/₁₆"
Use for Square in a Square.

 Cut 9 – 1⅞" x 1⅞"   *Cut once diagonally.*
Use for Square in a Square.

 Cut 9 – 1⅞" x 1⅞"   *Cut once diagonally.*
Use for Square in a Square.

 Make 9

 Cut 72 – 1½" x 1½"
Use for Flying Geese.

 Cut 36 – 1½" x 2½"
Use for Flying Geese.

 Make 36

Block Construction:

1. Row 1 – Sew together, as shown.
2. Row 2 – Sew together, as shown.
3. Row 3 – Sew together, as shown.
4. Press seams in direction of ⇄ .
5. Sew Rows 1, 2 & 3 together.
6. Press finished block.

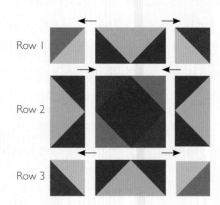

Row 1

Row 2

Row 3

Cutting Instructions for Sashing, 1st, 2nd Borders and Binding:

Sashing and corner stones:
Cut 12 strips – 1¼" × 4½" (brown)
Cut 4 squares - 1¼" × 1¼" (dark blue)

1st border:
Cut 2 strips – 1¼" × 14" (brown)
Cut 2 strips – 1¼" × 15½" (brown)

2nd border:
Cut 2 strips – 2" × 15½" (dark blue)
Cut 2 strips – 2" × 18½" (dark blue)

Quilt Construction:

1. Row 1 – Sew together, as shown.
2. Row 2 – Sew together, as shown.
3. Row 3 – Sew together, as shown.
4. Row 4 – Sew together, as shown.
5. Row 5 – Sew together, as shown.
6. Press seams in direction of ⇄ .
7. Press finished quilt body.

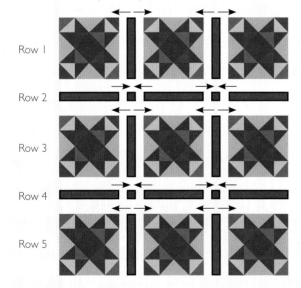

Row 1

Row 2

Row 3

Row 4

Row 5

Adding Borders:

(Refer to Fig. 1.)

1st border:
1. Sew strips to top and bottom of constructed quilt, as shown.
2. Sew strips to remaining sides of quilt, as shown.

2nd border:
1. Sew strips to top and bottom of 1st border, as shown.
2. Sew strips to remaining sides of 1st border, as shown.

Fig. 1

Finishing:

• Layer and quilt, using your favorite method.
• Binding. Cut 3 strips 2¼" × WOF (dark blue). Sew strips together, press wrong sides together, lengthwise.

Roses in the Cabin

20¼" x 20¼"

Add a touch of elegance to your table using a combination of appliqué and foundation paper piecing.

Materials:

Center Appliqué Square
- **Light Beige** – ⅓ yard (background)
- **Dark Green** – ¼ yard (circle stem)
- **Medium Green** – ⅛ yard (leaves)
- **Medium Red** – 6" × 6" (roses)
- **Dark Red** – 4" × 4" (rose centers)

Log Cabin Block
- **Medium Red** – ⅛ yard
- **Light Beige** – ⅛ yard
- **Medium Beige** – ¼ yard
- **Dark Beige** – ¼ yard
- **Light Green** – ¼ yard
- **Medium Green** – ¼ yard
- **Dark Green** – ¼ yard

Binding
- **Medium Green** – ¼ yard

Backing – ¾ yard

Center Appliqué Square:

• Cut the background fabric to a 12" × 12" square. **This will be trimmed to 9½" x 9½" after you have completed the appliqué.**

Prepare the appliqué pieces, using your favorite appliqué method.

There are various types of appliqué to choose from:
- • Traditional hand appliqué
- • Fusible web appliqué
- • Machine appliqué

Using the diagram as guide, arrange appliqué pieces as shown. Center ring should be appliquéd first. Proceed with flowers and leaves.

Striped Borders:

Step 1: Cut 2 strips 1½" × WOF (width of fabric) of each color: light beige, medium red and dark green.
Step 2: Sew 1 of each fabric (beige, red, green) together as shown. Press in direction of arrows.
Step 3: From strip sets cut 4 units 3½" × 17".

Make 4 units.

Corner Units:

Step 1: Cut 1 strip 1½" × WOF of each color: light beige and medium red.
Step 2: Sew strips together. Press in direction of ⇄ .

Step 3: Cut 4 units 2½" × 7".

Make 4 units.

Foundation Log Cabin:

Note: Duplicated images may vary by copier or printer. Log Cabin block measures 3" finished.

Step 1: Make 8 copies of the Log Cabin foundation page. This will give you a total of 28 blocks plus 4 extra, if needed.
Step 2: From beige and green fabrics cut 2 strips, 1" × WOF. Cut more strips as needed. From medium red fabric, cut 1 strip 2" × WOF.
Step 3: Using paper foundation, piece 28 blocks with beige fabrics on one half and green fabrics on the other. Darkest fabrics should be on outside, lightest on inside with red fabric in center.
Step 4: Sew 28 Log Cabin blocks on foundation paper.

Table Topper Construction:

Step 1: Sew set of 3 Log Cabin blocks together as shown.

Make 4   Make 2
Refer to picture for correct layout.

Step 2: Sew 5 Log Cabin blocks together as shown.

Make 2
Refer to picture for correct layout.

Step 3: Refer to layout for construction.

Step 4: Trim topper on lines, as shown.

NOTE: BE
CAREFUL NOT
TO STRETCH
THE EDGES,
THEY ARE CUT
ON THE BIAS!

Finishing:

- Layer and quilt, using your favorite method.
- Binding. Cut 3 strips 2¼" x WOF. Sew strips together, press wrong sides together, lengthwise.

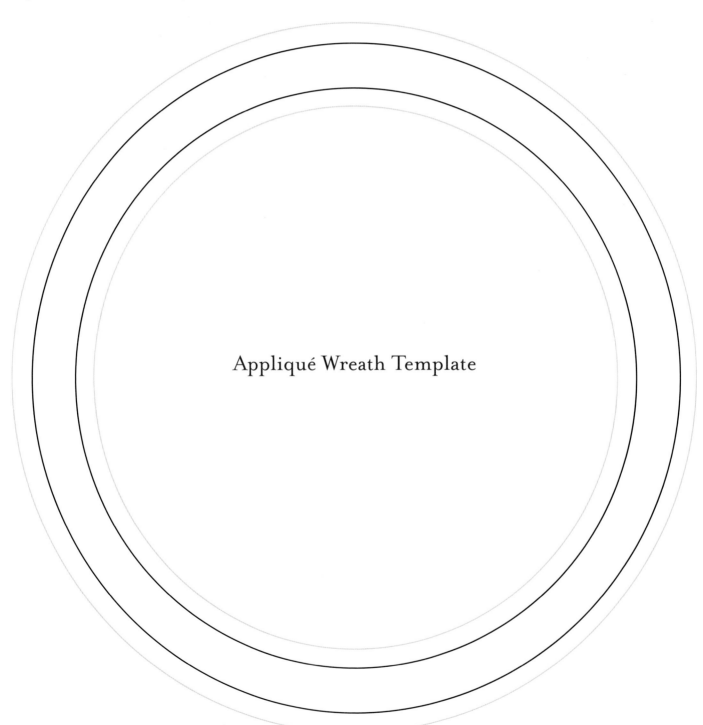

Appliqué Wreath Template

Cut 1

Cut 1

Cut 1

Cut 1

Cut 20

Cut 1

Cut 1

Cut 1

Cut 1

Log Cabin
3" × 3" finished

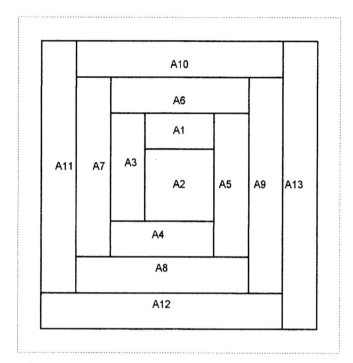

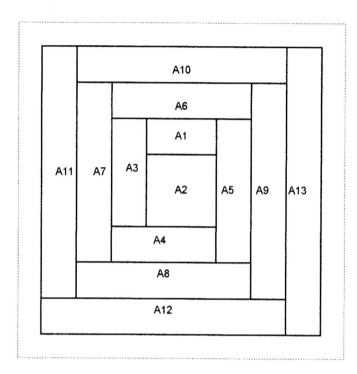

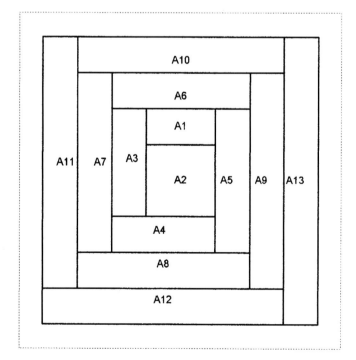

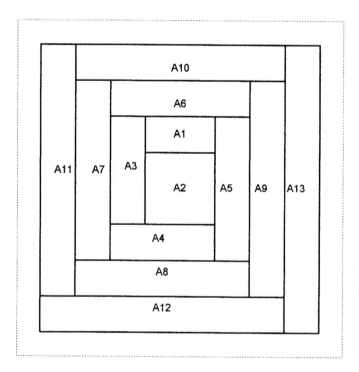

Barn quilts are typically hung on the exterior of barns, as the name implies. The directions for making an 8' x 8' barn quilt are provided. If you'd like a smaller version such as 4' x 4' or 2' x 2' to hang on the outside of an outbuilding, or garage or between 2 posts to make a sign, follow the directions provided for your preferred size quilt block.

Supplies:

- Plywood: 2 – 4' x 8' ¾" MDO for 8' x 8' finished barn quilt - or - 1 piece ¾" plywood cut to preferred size. Types of plywood:
  - MDO, sometimes called sign board, is engineered plywood with resin treated fiber applied to both sides. It's rated for exterior use, easy to paint, resistant to the elements. Call your local lumber yard for their stock.
  - Exterior plywood, also for exterior uses, is rated for the grade of surface on each side. For example: AB or AC. A: Smooth paintable finish; B: Some tight knots; C: Knotholes to 1".
- Drop cloth or plastic to cover floor
- Sawhorses or table
- Rulers, framing square, measuring tape
- Pencils (lead and colored) and crayons
- Self stick notes
- Paint
  - 100% acrylic latex primer
  - 100% semi-gloss acrylic latex enamel
- Paint stir sticks
- 2" paint brushes for Latex paint
- Foam rollers and paint tray
- Rags or paper towels
- Masking tape or painter's tape

Additional Supplies for Making 8' x 8' Barn Quilt:

- 6 – 8' cedar two-by-fours (used for borders and back bracing)
- Wood clamps
- Gorilla glue
- 1 – 4" x 8' tin piece (used for top cap)
- 8 "L" brackets and screws (used for hanging)
- 2" Torque screws (used to install "L" brackets on block)

Set up:

1. Cover floor surface with drop cloth or plastic.
2. Place plywood on top of sawhorses or table.

Prime:

1. Using foam roller, prime both sides and all edges of both plywood sheets using foam roller and primer.
2. Allow primer to dry thoroughly.

Design:

1. Select quilt block design or design your own. Draw design on graph paper. Make a few copies so you can color samples with crayons or colored pencils.
2. *Some helpful hints for 8' x 8' barn quilt:*
   a. Center seam of barn quilt (two plywood sheets aligned together) should run vertically. This will allow water runoff and reduce deterioration.
   b. Before you transfer block design to plywood, it may be helpful to *lightly* mark a 1' x 1' grid on plywood with lead pencil.

c. Two-by-fours will be added to perimeter of barn quilt which may be painted a contrasting color to form a border.

3. Display colored copy of your design in work area for handy reference.

4. Using lead pencil, rulers and framing square, mark quilt block design on plywood.

5. Mark each part of block design with self stick note indicating color it will be painted.

Paint:

1. Stir paint.

2. Starting with area that will be painted lightest color first, mark outline of area(s) with masking tape or painter's tape. Hint: Firmly press on all interior edges of tape to ensure good seal.

3. With a clean, dry foam roller, paint areas outlined in tape being careful not to paint outside taped area. You may need to repeat this step to ensure good paint coverage.

4. *Carefully* remove tape from plywood while paint is still wet. Hint: In an out-of-the-way place, hang up used tape, allow it to dry. Some tape which has a "fresh" edge (unpainted) may be reused.

5. Touch up areas where paint may have leaked.

6. Allow paint to dry *thoroughly* before taping and painting an adjacent area/color.

7. Repeat steps 1-7 with all design colors.

Border, Brace and Cap – for 8' x 8' Barn Quilt:

1. Prime and paint 4 cedar two-by-fours.

2. To make side borders, glue 1 two-by-four to each barn quilt side.

3. To make top and bottom borders, cut 2 two-by-fours to 7' 5". Glue to top and bottom of quilt block. Clamp all sides. Allow glue to dry.

4. Paint ends of borders with paint to match.

5. Make vertical brace by cutting 1 two-by-four to 7' 5". Glue in place over vertical seam (two pieces of plywood aligned together.) *Important:* Be sure corners of quilt design on quilt block front match.

6. Measure and cut 2 horizontal braces from remaining two-by-four. Place ends of cut two-by-four pieces against vertical two-by-four bracing. Glue in place.

7. Center tin strip on top border of quilt block. Bend one half of strip to each side of top border. Paint to match border.

8. *Using caution not to pierce front of quilt block*, screw 4 "L" brackets to top and bottom of quilt block using torque screws.

An 8' x 8' barn quilt may weigh 150 pounds. Consider inserting eye bolts in barn quilt top which may be used to hoist the block into position.

Apron Applause

When I was a child, Grandma's cover-all apron was a big affair of dark printed cotton, slow to soil, edged all around with bias tape. Its uses were limitless.

The apron made a "basket" when she gathered eggs from the henhouse. If there were fluffy, yellow chicks to be carried to the back porch during the sudden cold spells, they made the trip, peeping contentedly, in Grandma's apron. When these same little darlings grew into henhood and liked to scratch among Grandma's flowers, she merely flapped her apron at them and they ran squawking to the chicken yard.

Lots of chips and kindling were needed to start fires in the big ivory-colored cook stove in Grandma's kitchen. Sure, she carried them in her apron. Vegetables and fruits found their way to the kitchen via Grandma's carry-all. It was a handy holder for removing hot pans from the stove. If the men working in the field weren't too far away, the apron waved aloft was the signal to "come to dinner." At threshing time when the long dining room table was crowded with hungry folk, grandma hovered about, passing dishes and flipping the big apron at pesky flies.

When grandchildren came to visit, the apron stood ready to dry childish tears. If the little ones were a bit shy, it made a good place to hide in case a stranger appeared unexpectedly.

The apron was used countless times to stroke a perspiring brow as Grandma bent over the hot wood stove, or hoed the garden under a blistering sun. In chilly weather, Grandma wrapped the friendly apron around her arms while she hurried on an outside errand. It dusted tables and chairs if company was sighted coming down the lane. And, in the evening when the day's work was done, Grandma shed her garment of many uses and draped it over the canary's cage.

Reprinted from The Furrow,
Deere & Company,
(Dec. – Jan. 1955-1956)

Smock Apron

Embroidered
Gingham Apron
(on pages 76-78)

Fabric Requirements & Supplies:

- 1¾ yd. main fabric
- ⅓ yd. accent fabric (shoulder tabs, pockets, waist ties)
- 6⅔ yd. purchased bias binding

Or

- ¾ yd. accent fabric (to make bias binding, shoulder tabs, pockets, waist tie)
- 2 – 1⅜" decorative buttons

Cutting Instructions:

Main fabric (Fig.1) cut:

- 1 apron front and 1 apron back
- 2 waistbands (2½" × 16½")
- 4 waist ties (2½" × 12½")
- 2 shoulder tabs (2½" × 6½")
- 2 pockets (6½" × 6½")

Accent Fabric:

- 4 waist ties (2½" × 12½")
- 2 shoulder tabs (2½" × 6½")
- 2 pockets (6½" × 6½")
- 19" × 19" square for making 1¼" wide bias binding (6⅔ yd.)

Marking:

- Before unfolding apron pieces, mark waist gathers as shown (Fig. 1) on apron front and back.
- Place neck opening pattern (Fig. 9) at apron front top folded edge as shown (Fig. 1). Mark. Cut away. Repeat for apron back.
- Trace lower apron corner curve (Fig. 9) on apron front. Cut away. Repeat for apron back.

Important Notes:

- Fabric requirements based on 42" wide fabric.
- ¼" seam allowance, unless otherwise noted.
- Label all pattern pieces with name and dimensions as you cut.
- To resize pattern refer to Fig. 1.

Waist Ties:

- Layer waist tie to accent waist tie, RST. Sew 2 long sides and 1 short side. Trim corners, turn, RSO. Press.
- Topstitch on 3 sides. Repeat for remaining 3 waist ties. Set aside.

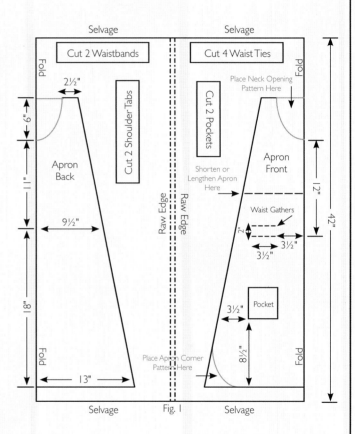

Fig. 1

Pockets:

- Layer pocket to accent pocket RST, sew all sides, leaving small opening on one side for turning. Trim corners, turn RSO. Press.
- Sew rickrack to pocket at top edge, turning under raw ends of rickrack (Fig. 2).
- Repeat for second pocket.
- Fold pocket top edge over 1" to pocket front side (Fig. 3). Press.
- Repeat for second pocket.
- Place pockets on apron as shown (Fig. 1). Topstitch in place on 3 sides.

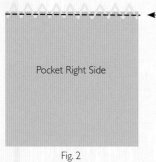

←— Stitching Line

Pocket Right Side

Fig. 2

Pocket Right Side

Fig. 3

Waist Gathers:

- Set basting stitch on sewing machine. Sew basting line between top and bottom markings on both sides of apron front. Gather. Adjust gathers so apron front measures 16½" wide. Repeat for apron back.

Waistband:

- Press under ¼" on both long waistband edges.
- Center wrong side of waistband over gathering stitches on right side of apron front. Pin in place. Pin waistband ends at edges of apron front.
- Slip rickrack under lower edge of waistband. Topstitch long waistband edges to apron.
- Repeat these steps for waistband back but do not add rick rack.

Waist Ties:

- Place raw edge of waist ties at raw edge of apron side, RST, centering waist tie on waistband. Finished end of waist tie should be facing toward body of apron. Baste raw edges with a scant ¼". Repeat for remaining 3 ties.
- Pin ties to apron body so they stay out of the way when sewing on binding.

Shoulder Tabs:

- Layer 1 shoulder tab to 1 accent shoulder tab, RST. Sew 2 long edges leaving openings at both ends. Press. Topstitch. (Fig. 4)
- Fold shoulder tabs in half, matching raw edges with main fabric inside. Baste raw edges together. (Fig. 5)

Apron Shoulder Assembly:

- Layer apron shoulder front to apron shoulder back, **wrong sides together.** Sew together at shoulder. (Fig. 6)
- Press seam allowances toward apron front.
- Pin raw edges of finished shoulder tab at shoulder seam stitching line. Folded edge of shoulder tab should face apron front. (Fig. 6)
- Make fold ½" in apron back, down from shoulder seam. Bring this fold over raw edges. (Fig. 7) Topstitch to apron front. (Fig. 8)

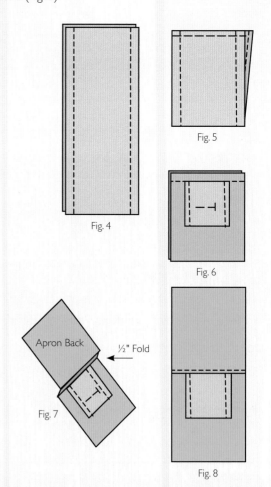

Fig. 5

Fig. 4

Fig. 6

Apron Back

½" Fold

Fig. 7

Fig. 8

Binding and Buttons:

Using homemade bias:

- Press under ¼" on one long edge of bias binding.
- Sew raw edge of bias to raw edge of apron and around apron neck opening, RST. Fold bias binding in half to inside. Machine or hand stitch in place.
- Fold shoulder tabs down against apron front. Secure in place with buttons.

Using readymade bias:

- Open out bias. Sew raw edge of bias to raw edge of apron and around apron neck opening, RST. Fold bias binding in half to inside. Machine or hand stitch in place.
- Fold shoulder tabs down against apron front. Secure in place with buttons.

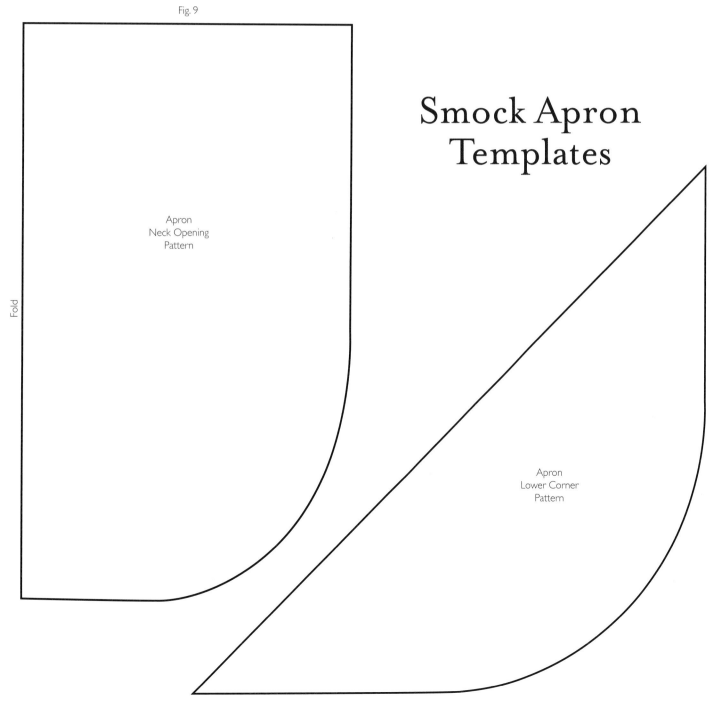

Fig. 9

Smock Apron Templates

Apron Neck Opening Pattern

Fold

Apron Lower Corner Pattern

Embroidered Gingham Apron

Fabric Requirements and Supplies:

- 1 yd. ⅛" gingham check fabric
- Embroidery floss:
  - 2 skeins color #1 (flowers)
  - 1 skein color #2 (inner flower border)
  - 1 skein color #3 (flower center)
- Embroidery hoop
- Embroidery needle
- Marking pen (vanishing or wash away)

> Gingham check dimensions may vary by fabric manufacturer.

Apron Construction:

Pocket:

- Fold pocket in half once and in half again to form a square. Mark center using vanishing marking pen. Using 3 strands of embroidery floss, embroider design (Fig. 1) on white gingham squares, working from center out. *Tip: For even-looking embroidery, always keep right slanting half cross stitches on bottom and left slanting half cross stitches on top.*

- Trim pocket to 7¼" high × 6" wide (centering design). Press ¼" to inside on all pocket sides. Top stitch one short side (pocket top.)

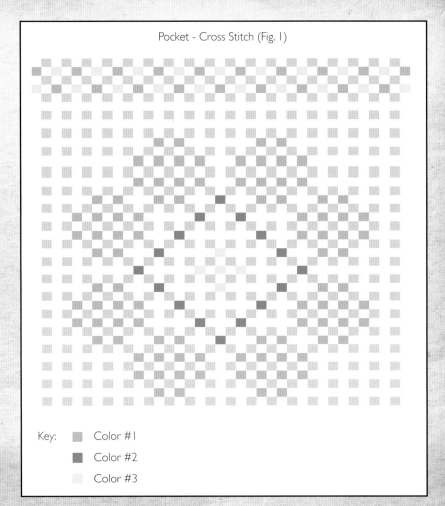

Pocket - Cross Stitch (Fig. 1)

Key:
- ▨ Color #1
- ▨ Color #2
- ▨ Color #3

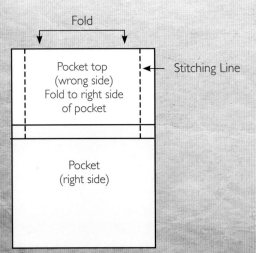

Fold

Pocket top
(wrong side)
Fold to right side
of pocket

Stitching Line

Pocket
(right side)

Fig. 2

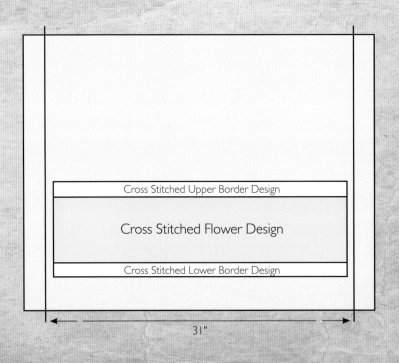

Cross Stitched Upper Border Design

Cross Stitched Flower Design

Cross Stitched Lower Border Design

31"

Fig. 4

- Turn 1¼" pocket top hem to right side of pocket. Stitch ends of pocket top hem (Fig.2). Clip corners. Turn RSO.

- Press remaining pocket edges ¼" to inside.

- Position pocket top 4½" from apron skirt top and 2½" from right apron skirt side. Topstitch pocket to apron skirt.

Cutting Instructions:

- 1 apron skirt (24" × WOF) Use gingham check design as cutting line on top and bottom apron edges.

- 2 apron ties (3" × 28")

- 1 waistband (2¾" × 17¼")

- 1 pocket (9½" × 8½")

Apron Skirt:

- Press ¼" bottom apron skirt edge to wrong side. Topstitch. Press under 2" to wrong side to form apron hem. Hand baste in place. Working from apron skirt center to both apron sides, cross stitch lower border design to hold apron hem in place (Fig. 3).

- Fold apron skirt in half (width). Mark center. Working from apron skirt center to both apron sides, cross stitch 7 flowers and top border design (Fig. 3). 3³/₈" flower design = 15 white gingham squares. Adjust flower spacing across apron skirt for your size gingham check. *Very Important: Flower design/upper border cross stitch design should line up with lower border cross stitch design as shown in Fig 3.*

- Cut away both apron skirt sides 1" beyond widest cross stitch design (Fig 4). Press ¼" to inside on both apron skirt sides ¼". Turn under ¼" again. Press. Topstitch.

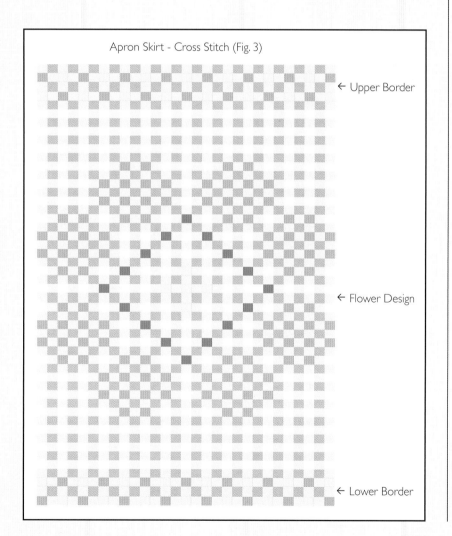

Apron Skirt - Cross Stitch (Fig. 3)

← Upper Border

← Flower Design

← Lower Border

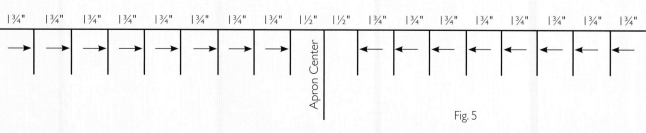

Fig. 5

Waist Pleats:

- Apron skirt top should measure 31". Fold width of apron skirt in half. Mark apron top center. From center, out to both apron skirt sides, make marks at:
1½", 1¾", 1¾", 1¾", 1¾", 1¾", 1¾", 1¾", 1¾"

- Refer to Fig 5. Working from each apron skirt side to apron center on wrong side of apron skirt, make folds in direction of arrows. (Fig. 5). Waist should measure 16¼" at this point.

- Baste across apron top to hold pleats in place. Baste each pleat 2" vertically. Use gingham check as guide to be sure pleats are even in depth and parallel to one another.

Waistband:

- Press ¼" to inside on one long edge. Edgestitch.

- Mark waistband center. Mark apron center.

- Working from center, pin long raw waistband edge to top apron edge, matching centers. Waistband will extend about ½" beyond each apron edge. Stitch. Press seam allowances toward waistband.

- Fold waistband ends to inside so waistband edges are even with apron edge. Press. Fold waistband to inside of apron. Baste long waistband edge to apron skirt.

- Cross stitch apron top design to hold waistband in place (Fig. 6).

Apron Waist - Cross Stitch (Fig. 6)

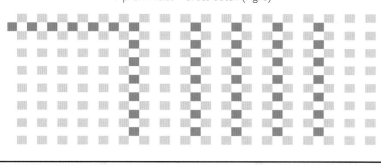

Ties:

- Press ¼" to inside on one long edge of each tie. Turn under ¼" again. Topstitch. Press under ¼" on second long edge.

- To make angled tie end: With tie right side facing up, fold tie end at 45° angle, matching tie end raw edge with tie pressed edge. Stitch tie end raw edge/tie pressed edge with a ¼" seam allowance, backstitching at both ends (Fig. 7). Trim corner. Turn tie end RSO. Press and topstitch edge.

- Repeat for second tie. Important: Second tie end angle should be a mirror image of first tie end angle.

- Cross stitch apron end design about 2 ½" from end of tie (Fig. 8).

Finishing

- Tuck raw tie end in opening at apron top on each apron skirt side. *Important: Be sure angled apron ends are facing in opposite directions.*

- Edgestitch both apron skirt edges to hold ties in place.

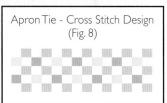

Apron Tie - Cross Stitch Design (Fig. 8)

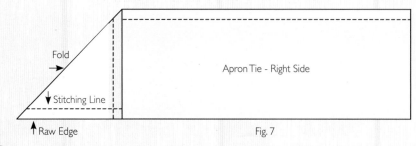

Fold

Stitching Line

Raw Edge

Apron Tie - Right Side

Fig. 7

Barns are about as inherent to America's rural landscape as buildings can be. They just plain belong there. Tucked away in the countryside, most of them go unnoticed; perhaps we're oblivious because we've seen so many.

Too often, these impressive structures that embody our history and culture are abandoned or rendered obsolete by current farming methods. They've outlived their usefulness. Past their prime, they languish, teetering in the wind. The gigantic task of preserving them is nearly impossible without huge investments. Such was the case of the Teeple Barn in Elgin, Illinois.

Lester Teeple, an early settler in Elgin, wanted to build an octagonal barn, which was characteristic among Flemish immigrants in that region. The lumber he planned to use wasn't long enough to construct a building with eight sides, so Teeple did all he could conceive in that circumstance: he built a structure with sixteen sides. Designed by local architect W. Wright Abell in 1885, the 13,500 square foot dairy barn measured 85 feet in diameter and 80 feet tall. It had a floor of locally-fired brick, laid on a stone foundation. Teeple hired men from town to build the barn for $1.00 a day.

The barn remained in the Teeple family for over 100 years. It was listed in the National Register of Historic Places in 1979. Ag-Tech, a non-profit group, raised $300,000 to make limited repairs to the barn, including restoration of the barn's cupola in 1999. The cost to restore the barn completely was estimated at more than $1 million.

On May 25, 2007, the historic barn succumbed to high winds. Its remains were demolished a few days later.

Ref: Ken & Carroll Teeple, Ref: ARCHITECT (magazine), July 2007

Supplies:

- 10" x 12" – 28 count linen, stitched over 2 threads
- Embroidery hoop
- Floss – refer to key

Directions:

1. To prevent fabric from fraying, bind edges with masking tape or zig-zag stitch fabric edges.
2. For best results, use embroidery hoop.
3. Determine center of fabric and center of design.
4. Use two strands of floss for cross stitches.
5. Secure thread by holding one inch of thread behind fabric and secure with the first few stitches, or run needle and thread under several stitches and take a small backstitch. To finish a thread, run needle and thread under four or more stitches on back of design.
6. Work all cross stitches before doing backstitch or straight stitch outlines. Backstitch on roof and on barn base is done with one strand 839. Straight stitch around windows and doors is done in two strands 3033. Straight stitch in center of windows is done in one strand 3033.
7. After all stitching is complete, wash embroidery and iron smooth. Frame as desired.

Finished design size 3½" x 5½"

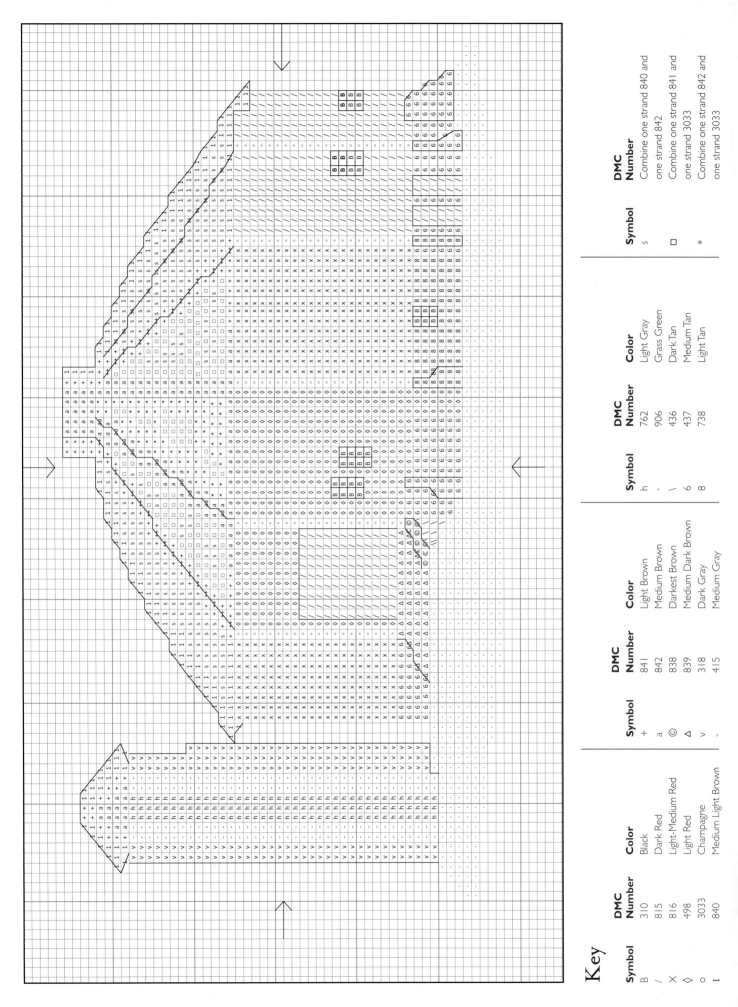

Key

Symbol	DMC Number	Color
B	310	Black
/	815	Dark Red
X	816	Light-Medium Red
◇	498	Light Red
o	3033	Champagne
1	840	Medium Light Brown

Symbol	DMC Number	Color
+	841	Light Brown
a	842	Medium Brown
◎	838	Darkest Brown
◁	839	Medium Dark Brown
v	318	Dark Gray
-	415	Medium Gray

Symbol	DMC Number	Color
h	762	Light Gray
.	906	Grass Green
\	436	Dark Tan
6	437	Medium Tan
8	738	Light Tan

Symbol	DMC Number
s	Combine one strand 840 and one strand 842
□	Combine one strand 841 and one strand 3033
*	Combine one strand 842 and one strand 3033

Dishtowel Embroidery Instructions:

Trace daisy design 3" from dishtowel edges at one corner using light box. (Make sure to mark towel very lightly.) Embroider design with 2 strands of floss.

Fabric trimmed edge:

1. Cut off all dishtowel hemmed edges. Make sure corners are squared off at 90°. Measure perimeter.
2. Main fabric trim: Cut strips at 2¼" × WOF. Total strip length should be 8"-10" longer than dishtowel perimeter. Connect strip short ends together at a 45° angle. Trim. Press seams open. Fold trim in half lengthwise matching long (raw) edges. Press.
3. Accent fabric trim: Cut 4 strips 1" × WOF. Do not sew strips together. Fold trim in half lengthwise matching long (raw) edges. Press.
4. Sew main fabric trim to wrong side of dishtowel with accurate ¼", leaving fabric tail at beginning to finish trim ends. Miter corners. Finish trim ends. Clip excess towel and trim at corners. Press seam allowance toward trim.
5. Lay bound dishtowel on flat surface (table for example). Place long raw edges of accent trim at main fabric/dishtowel sewing line. Folded edge of accent trim should face body of dishtowel and one short end of accent trim should lay adjacent to sewing line at right towel edge. Cut other accent trim end off at sewing line of left towel edge. (Fig. 1) Repeat this step for remaining towel edges.

Fabric Requirements and Supplies:

- ⅔ yd. main fabric (outer trim)
- ⅛ yd. accent fabric (inner trim)

- Floss: (DMC) #728 daisies; #580 stems and leaves; #938 daisy centers and French knots
- Embroidery hoop
- Pigma pen – size 01 or mechanical pencil
- Light box

Main Fabric

Dishtowel
Front Side

Trim Accent Fabric Here

Folded Edge

Fig. 1

Dishtowel
Front Side

Mitered Corner

Fig. 2

6. Fold main fabric trim up over dishtowel raw edges toward right side of towel. Dishtowel raw edges should be at main fabric folded edge (inside). Pin. Machine stitch main fabric trim to dishtowel. (Fig. 2) Tip: use a stiletto to adjust main fabric binding width or accent trim as necessary. Press finished towel.

Fabric Requirements and Supplies:

- Towel fabric (22" x 25") or ready-made hand towel
- 1/8 yd. accent fabric
- Fabric scraps for flowers
- Fabric scraps for yo-yos (flower centers)
- Fusible web
- 3 – 1" buttons
- 1 skein embroidery floss

Directions:

1. Press ½" to inside on both long sides and 1 short end of towel fabric. Turn under ½" again. Press. Topstitch. (If using ready-made towel, skip this step).
2. Cut accent fabric 22" x 4". (If using ready-made towel, cut accent fabric 4" wide x 2" larger than towel width.)
3. RST, lay accent fabric on towel 2¾" up from bottom of towel. Accent trim should extend 1" beyond sides of towel. Stitch with ¼" seam. (Fig. 1) Press accent fabric down over towel. Topstitch along seam on right side. (Fig. 2)

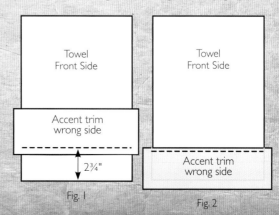

Fig. 1 — Towel Front Side / Accent trim wrong side / 2¾"

Fig. 2 — Towel Front Side / Accent trim wrong side

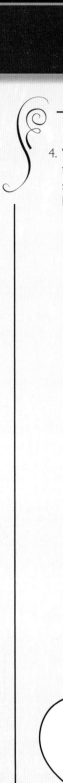

4. Working from back side of towel, press ½" of accent fabric to inside on long edge of accent trim and both short ends of accent trim. (Fig. 3) Turn under ½" again. Miter at corners. Press. Topstitch. (Fig.4)

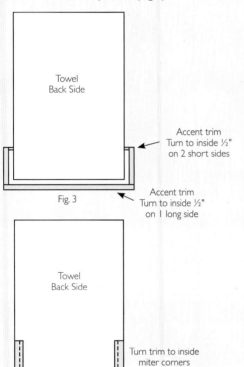

Towel
Back Side

Accent trim
Turn to inside ½"
on 2 short sides

Fig. 3

Accent trim
Turn to inside ½"
on 1 long side

Towel
Back Side

Turn trim to inside
miter corners

Fig. 4

5. Trace appliqué flower designs onto fusible web. Fuse web to flower fabrics. Fuse flowers to towel as shown in photo.
6. Machine or hand blanket stitch around flowers.
7. Yo-yo (flower center): trace yo-yo on flower center fabric, using circle template provided. Thread needle with single thread. Knot. Baste ⅛" (small even stitches) from edge around entire perimeter of circle cut-out. (Fig. 5) Pull basting thread slowly until you have gathered stitches and circle has become a little pouf. Be sure right side of fabric is on outside of yo-yo. Secure thread with knot.

Fig. 5

8. Center yo-yo on fused flower with raw edges facing up. Sew buttons to yo-yo center, covering gathers.
9. Using 6 strands embroidery floss, embroider evenly spaced lines on accent trim as shown in photo.

Yo-Yo Pattern
3½" diameter

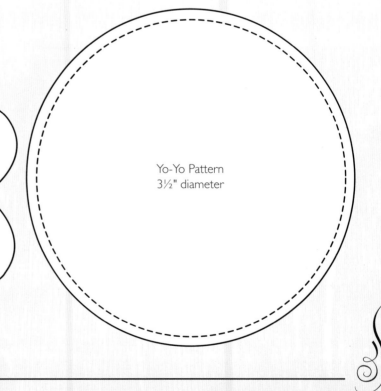

Yo-Yo Pattern
3½" diameter

Quilts are storytellers—remnants of life pieced together in beautiful patterns that speak of baby bonnets and Easter dresses, bathroom curtains and Christmas tree skirts. They help us picture relatives we have never met. They teach us about patience and friendship, tradition and heritage while they cover our beds, our chairs, and the people we love. As a whole, they help define us by holding in trust our most cherished memories. —Debbie Salter Goodwin, *Quilted with Love.* Reprinted with permission.

Many of us have passed time identifying memorable fabric scraps while lying under an old family quilt. These colorful remembrances provided warmth for years before they were handed down. Today, they link us to our past.

Now and then a quilt may hold an extraordinary story, or have an item such as a state fair ribbon or newspaper clipping that accompanies it. To ensure these items aren't separated from the quilt, you can sew a pocket to the quilt back. Write the quilt's story or tuck identifying documents inside—but be sure to remove them before the quilt is laundered. Anyone who receives the quilt will be grateful for the background that makes it a bit of living history.

Fabric Requirements and Supplies:

Single color pocket:
• ¼ yd. pocket fabric
• 1 button

Multi-color pocket:
• ¼ yd. pocket fabric
• ¼ yd. pocket accent fabric
• 1 button

This project is suitable for fat eighths or 6" x 10" fabric scraps. Quilt label pocket size may be altered to fit your need.

Directions:

Both pockets are sewn using a ¼" seam allowance.

Single color pocket:
• Cut 2 pocket fabric pieces 6" x 10".
• With RST, stitch around pocket fabric, leaving 2" opening for turning (Fig. 1.)
• Clip corners. Turn right side out. Press.
• Fold bottom end of pocket up 2½". Stitch edges (Fig. 2.)
• Make buttonhole in pocket flap (Fig. 2.)
• Sew button on pocket through outer pocket layer only.
• Hand stitch pocket on all sides to quilt back.

Multi-color pocket:
• Cut 1 6" x 10" from pocket fabric.
• Cut 1 6" x 10" from pocket accent fabric.
• With RST, stitch short pocket ends (Fig. 3.) Press seams open. Treat this piece as a tube or cylinder; manipulate so the 2 seams match or flatten with seams matched.
• Stitch pocket sides, leaving 2" opening on one side for turning (Fig. 4.)
• Clip corners. Turn right side out. Press.
• Fold bottom end of pocket up 2½". Stitch edges (Fig. 5.)
• Make buttonhole in pocket flap (Fig. 5.)
• Sew button on pocket through outer pocket layer only.
• Hand stitch pocket on all sides to quilt back.

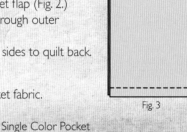

Multi-Color Pocket

Fig. 3

Single Color Pocket

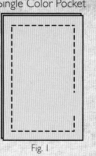

Fig. 1

Fig. 4

Fold

Fig. 2

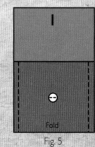

Fold

Fig. 5

St. Peter's Evangelical Lutheran Church
Union, Minnesota

St. Peter's Evangelical Lutheran Church was founded in 1868, a brief ten years after Minnesota became the 32nd of the United States. At that time, Pastor Friedrich Reitz conducted monthly services in a schoolhouse shared with the Reformed Church of America, Methodists and Baptists. Feeling a bit crowded, in 1870 the eight-family Lutheran congregation built for itself a modest frame church just outside the Caledonia, Minnesota community nearby.

The St. Peter's congregation had grown to 40 families by 1895, when fire destroyed the beloved church building, parsonage and all the church records. Controversy arose amongst the congregation because some members thought the church should be rebuilt in Caledonia, while others wanted the church to remain in Union Township, four miles northeast of Caledonia. In the end, the congregation divided evenly: half the families opened St. John's Evangelical Lutheran Church in Caledonia, and the other half rebuilt St. Peter's Evangelical Lutheran Church in Union Township. The same minister, Pastor John C. Siegler served both congregations. A group of St. Peter's faithful, 27 communicants from seven families, worshiped weekly at the quaint country church into the 1980s. Today, a few considerate citizens respectfully maintain the church grounds and adjoining cemetery.

As sure as an old barn on a family farm evokes memories of times long gone, this retired country church reminds us of the faithful who gathered there in times past.

Ref. History of Houston County, 1982, provided by Houston County Historical Society.

Harvest Table Blessing

Thank you, Lord, for the abundance of nature;
For the labor of those who plant,
harvest and prepare;
For health and appetite to enjoy Thy bounty
And for all who gather around this table.
May this food and fellowship
Give us strength we need
To carry out your work in the world.

Amen

*The League of Catholic Women,
Minneapolis, MN*